2-24-68

Your Church and Your Community

Huber F. Klemme

Your Church and Your Community

Published for the Co-operative Publication Association

CHRISTIAN EDUCATION PRESS · Philadelphia

The Co-operative Series
Leadership Training Texts

Many thousands of lay workers in Protestant churches attend interdenominational leadership education schools each year. It is essential that the courses offered and the text materials used be acceptable to the many varieties of Protestant groups found in our American communities.

The Co-operative Series of leadership education textbooks are produced to meet that need. They are planned by the Division of Christian Education of the National Council of the Churches of Christ in the U.S.A., representing thirty-nine Protestant denominations. The Co-operative Publication Association, an interdenominational group of denominational editors and publishers, selects the writers and provides editorial supervision to insure sound educational values, practical usefulness, and interdenominational approval and acceptance.

Copyright 1957

THE CHRISTIAN EDUCATION PRESS

Library of Congress Catalog Card Number: 57-10956

1133035

TO MIRIAM

who in home, church, and school
serves the Beloved Community

CHAPTER ONE

The Church Has a Community Responsibility

THIS STUDY BEGINS with the assumption that the church—meaning your church, any local church—has a responsibility for the community in which it is situated. Our chief interest will be in examining certain aspects of that responsibility and some of the ways in which it can be met.

But has the church such a responsibility? Although most thoughtful Christians would undoubtedly agree, there are some who are not certain and others who would deny that the church is in any special way concerned about the problems of the community.

On the one hand, there are some church people, purporting to have the interest of religion at heart, who say, "Religion is a matter of the individual. The church ministers to the individual human soul. It has no concern with society as such."

On the other hand, there are some individuals who, speaking from the point of view of community agencies and other social institutions, belittle the church's community function. "Concentrate your efforts on the human soul," they say in effect; "we will take care of the social needs." One is reminded of the song, "Anything you can do, I can do better!"

Strangely enough this argument—whether it comes from pious exponents of individual religion, from individuals who exploit their neighbors, or from a few unsympathetic educators or social workers—reminds one of the attitude frequently reported by visitors to countries dominated by Communist governments. There, too, the church is expected to confine its ministrations to the crises in the personal life of its members; and its leaders do not acknowledge any obligation to deal with basic relationships in the community. One can appreciate the restrictions placed upon the church's field of action under a totalitarian regime, and the courage required to maintain any sort of Christian witness in such a situation. But one cannot accept indifference to the problems of community as normal and right where the church is free.

As against those who on either secularistic or religious grounds assume the church has no social concern, we must keep in mind four important considerations:

1. *The church is concerned with persons.* Each man and woman is precious in the sight of God. As Jesus said, "There is joy before the angels of God over one!" This is emphasized even by those who discount the social task. But persons do not live in one-man space-ships separated from each other by millions of miles. They live in more or less intimate association with other persons, in families, groups, communities, and associations of various kinds. They are profoundly affected by com-

munity conditions, institutions, and experiences. If they are deprived of important freedoms by a dictatorship, they may rise to spiritual greatness; but this does not make dictatorship a good thing. So, for a child to be surrounded by drunkenness and vice tolerated or encouraged by the community may distort or injure his personality for life. Slum living, racial segregation, economic injustice, lack of opportunity for education, or other pressures may have serious effects upon the lives of human beings. Simply because the church is concerned with persons, with *every* person, the church is concerned with whatever affects their welfare. And that means the church has a responsibility for its community.

2. *The church is entrusted with a gospel.* Oddly enough, some persons object to the church dealing with social issues on the ground that it should "stick to the gospel." But the gospel of Christ is concerned with all men and with the whole of life. God is the Creator of the whole world, the Sovereign Lord of all. "God so loved the world that he gave his Son!" His redemptive love extends to every man. His Spirit strives to penetrate and sanctify all man's relationships. The gospel which offers wholeness to individual persons, offers the possibility for the fulfillment of our corporate life in society. In faithfulness to this gospel, the church can admit no "No Trespassing" signs. This does not mean that the church must itself operate or control all agencies and institutions in the community. It does not mean that it is equally responsible for every imaginable service, or ought not establish certain priorities. It does mean that the church cannot abdicate its social function. It has a special responsibility for seeing that the deepest needs are met, that the needs which are otherwise overlooked are kept before men's minds, that the "downmost" men are not forgotten, and that—however good or bad a given society may be—a critical Christian judgment is maintained toward every situation. Other agencies may rightly share in fulfilling these aims, but no other institution can relieve the church of that obligation.

3. *The church inevitably affects the community*. As Muriel S. Webb has put it: "The local church cannot decide whether or not it is to affect the life of its community. It does so by its very existence; by its physical presence; by the nature of its worship, teaching, and work; and by the everyday activity of its members. It can decide whether the results will be negative or positive, small or great, decisive or ineffective."[1] Its very failure to use its influence constructively may cause a community to suffer. Some years ago Dr. E. L. Thorndyke studied a number of American cities and found that those which had the highest number of churches and church members rated lowest in their expenditures for public education, public recreation, and other indications of social health!

4. *Conversely, a church cannot ignore the life of its community, for the community also affects the church*. Lawless-

---

[1] Muriel S. Webb, *The Social Ministry of the Local Church*, p. 9. Department of Social Welfare, National Council of the Churches of Christ in the U.S.A., 1956.

ness and delinquency unheeded and uncombated, directly or indirectly take their toll of the children, the youth,
and the youth program of the church. A church that fails
to minister to its new neighbors in a period of population
change may find itself struggling for its life. Even a new
highway or industrial development may precipitate a
crisis. Institutional self-preservation is not the best reason for undertaking a community ministry, but it may
force a congregation to become aware of its community.

Thus the problem is not *whether* the church has a
community task or not, but how that obligation is going
to be discharged—whether wisely, responsibly, purpose-
fully, effectively, or not. For the life to which Christians
are called in the church is a life of social responsibility
and loving service. The Christian community is de-
scribed as *light,* as *salt,* as *the body of Christ.* These are
terms which denote usefulness, influence, action. The
Christian is called to be a *witness,* a *disciple,* and a good
steward of his resources and influence. These terms suggest the dynamic relation between himself, his Lord, and
his fellow men. The very fact of his calling indicates
that he is on a mission for his Lord, a mission which always moves beyond self to others in the family, the
community, and the world.

The New Testament tells us that when Jesus called
the Twelve he appointed them "to be with him, and
to be sent out to preach and have authority to cast out
demons" (Mark 3:14f). So the Christian today must seek
the fellowship of Christ, must strive to win others to
him, and must in the spirit of the Lord help to heal
men. And the church, too, must worship, must proclaim

the gospel, and must "cast out demons" whether they afflict the individual person or persons in large groups. That is to say, it must serve the needs of the whole man and the needs of the whole community. This is our charter for a complete ministry in our time.

The Responsibility of the Church

It will be clear from what has been said that while the church is responsible *for* the well-being of the community, it is not responsible *to* the community. Basically, it is responsible to the Lord himself. Since the Son of Man came among us as One who serves, and he has commanded us to love one another as he has loved us, the church exists in the community as the *servant* of the community. But it is not an uncritical servant, doing the bidding of whatever forces are in control. It is also the *critic* of the community, subjecting all decisions and arrangements to prophetic judgment, stimulating the conscience of the community, and encouraging action to correct what is evil or improve what is good but not good enough.

How these two approaches interact is illustrated in a passage from the booklet already referred to:

> The church has always served and still serves as the social conscience of the community, setting the moral goals for its life, and fostering within individuals the will to help others.
>
> Because of its historic role as the founder of social services, the church created much of the pattern for many voluntary services as they are carried on today.
>
> Because of its belief in the Incarnation, the church has always been one of the prime integrating forces in the

community, firmly supporting the unity of all life, spiritual, physical, mental, social, economic, and political.

Because of its belief in the sacredness of human personality, the church holds fast to the value of each individual and, in a time when mass impersonal living threatens this value, still stands ready to support the sacredness of each person in the sight of God.

The church corporately and through its members expresses Christ's judgment upon the sins of society and his command for social justice for all.

The church witnesses to the need of all men for a social ministry, not only the need of those who seem to be disadvantaged, but of everyone no matter what his economic or social position.[2]

To these may be added that the church, as the local representative of the Church Universal, lifts men's sights and stretches their horizons so that they participate in the life of the world community, working for peace with justice among the nations.

Perhaps the relationship between the church and its community can be illustrated *negatively* by two experiences reported to the writer. In the one instance, a friend visited a well-known church with a large plant, a large budget, a wealthy membership, and a variety of activities ranging from psychology classes to dancing lessons. However, neither the ideas expressed in the pulpit nor the influence exerted by the members bore any prophetic Christian imprint. The church simply reflected the interests of the comfortable people of that city.

In the other instance, a minister came to the pastorate of an established congregation. He found the usual pro-

---

[2] *Ibid.,* p. 10.

gram—Sunday services, church school, Lenten services, organizations—and a fairly loyal, scattered membership. But the community did not even know the church was there. A neighboring businessman did not recognize the name of the church when the new pastor introduced himself. It had been in the neighborhood but had been isolated from it.

Neither a church that is conformed to its community nor one that is irrelevant to it will do. We seek a church that inspires the truest service and the highest standards, a friend that is both servant and critic—neither a social club nor a hermitage, but a leaven!

The Community

Strictly speaking, the term "community" applies to any grouping or association of people bound together by some common purpose, function, ideal, or cohesive force. Thus there are communities of work, of learning, of kinship, and of faith as well as the geographical communities to which we usually refer when we use the term. All these communities—and others—intersect one another at many points, and all of us belong to many of them at once.

The "household of faith"—the church—is itself a community within these other communities. Its members are bound together by the most solemn tie of all, their common calling by their common Lord to a common fellowship and service. Its membership embraces the faithful in all lands, organized in many local congregations and denominations.

The local church, too, is a community—a more intimate community—within which ideally all members partake of a common life by which each is strengthened and sustained. Its membership, too, may be scattered in many sections of a city, across wide stretches of open country, indeed to far places where individual members serve in posts of duty as soldiers, businessmen, technicians, ambassadors, missionaries, or employees of various enterprises.

But in this study we are thinking most of all of the local church's relation to its immediate geographical environment and the people within it. For if a church has any reason for being and any reason for existing in a certain location defined and typified usually by a building in which it gathers for worship, instruction, and fellowship, *it has a responsibility for the people within and without its fellowship who reside immediately around the place where its life is focused.* It may minister to people beyond the immediate vicinity of its church building, and it may divide its neighborhood ministry with one, two, or more neighboring congregations of the same or of different denominational affiliation. But it cannot ignore that community—the natural "parish" for which it needs to offer, in so far as it possibly can, the resources of worship, evangelistic outreach, Christian education, Christian fellowship, and a Christian social ministry as well.

Your Church and Its Community

How will you determine the specific community for which your particular congregation is responsible? This will depend upon a number of factors. If yours is a large city, there may be a "natural" neighborhood, determined by such boundaries as major thoroughfares, railroad lines, parks, industrial areas, or rivers, or other bodies of water. Most large cities are divided into census tracts, and these may correspond to parish boundaries. City plan commissions or social planning councils may have determined where the communities within the larger community lie. If none of these can help you, draw a circle with a radius of a mile, with your church as the center, noting the major traffic arteries which set off one neighborhood from the next, and thus center your responsibility area.

If you are in a small town or village, your parish may include not simply the village itself but a good share of the surrounding countryside. Local merchants, service club leaders, or county agents can probably suggest where the natural "trading area" of the community lies. Or the location of the bulk of your members will help determine your field of major responsibility. The same principle applies if your church is in the open country.

In either case, unless your church is in the unusual position of being the only community church, there will be other churches sharing the field with you. In many instances you may be able to cooperate effectively both in studying and in serving the community. Sometimes it may even be possible for each congregation to specialize in a different needed service. We shall consider this in the closing chapter. For the present we are concerned to locate and begin the study of the specific area in which your congregation lies. You cannot serve your community if you do not know it!

Studying Your Community

There are a number of guides for surveying the moral and social needs of the community. Probably the most exhaustive guide to such analysis in virtually every area is *Studying Your Community* by Roland L. Warren, published by the Russell Sage Foundation. An excellent Outline for a Church-Community Survey is found in the appendix of Professor Harvey Seifert's *The Church in Community Action,* published by Abingdon-Cokesbury. This book is a first-rate guide for any church in facing up to its social opportunities.

For groups which cannot for the present take time to engage in an exhaustive study and for readers who do not have access to these more elaborate survey guides, the following outline is suggested, each question being followed by a list of some of the kinds of agencies which could be helpful in providing the information desired:

1. WHAT IS YOUR COMMUNITY? What is the extent and what are the boundaries of your natural geographical "parish"? What are its chief characteristics? To what extent is it residential, commercial, industrial, agricultural? What are its traditions and significant action patterns?

United States Census Bureau (census tract data), city planning commission, chamber of commerce, school board.

2. WHO LIVES HERE? How many people are there? What is the density of the population, its economic, ethnic, age, sex, and educational distribution? How long have the residents lived here? How fast are they moving in or out? How large are the family units? What is the birth rate? What are the rates of divorce and legal separation?

United States Census Bureau (census tract data), council of social agencies, chamber of commerce, central labor councils.

3. WHAT KINDS OF HOMES DO PEOPLE LIVE IN? What percentage of the families own their own homes? What do these homes cost? What is the cost and condition of rental housing? Is there overcrowding? How many people per room? Are there hotels, rooming houses, trailer camps, and other facilities which mean transiency? Is there need for slum clearance and low-cost housing?

United States Census Bureau (census tract data), housing authorities, city zoning board, real estate board, council of social agencies; in rural communities: county farm agent, farm bureau, extension service of state university.

4. WHAT IS THE ECONOMIC CHARACTER OF THE COMMUNITY? What is the income range of the people? How do they make their living? What problems do they face in their daily work? What is the relation between labor and management, businessman and consumer, farmer and townsman? Is any economic group insufficiently represented in the leadership of the churches?

State department of labor, public employment service, chamber of commerce, labor organizations.

5. WHAT ARE THE SCHOOLS LIKE? What sort of educational facilities are provided? What standards prevail? What are the chief needs or problems of the schools? Are equal privileges open to all children of the community without discrimination? What opportunities for education are offered to adults and young people after they leave school?

State and local boards of education, PTA, public school personnel.

6. HOW IS THE COMMUNITY GOVERNED? What is the status of law enforcement and the administration of justice? What are the facts about crime and delinquency? What provision is made for the treatment and rehabilitation of offenders? What measures are taken, or needed, to prevent delinquency? How fully do citizens participate in the processes of government? Are civil rights and civil liberties adequately protected?

Charter of local municipality, county and city annual reports, municipal research department, police department, juvenile court.

7. WHAT IS THE STATE OF THE COMMUNITY'S HEALTH? Who gets sick, and why? What are the birth and death rates per thousand? What provision is made for treating contagious disease? for improving mental health? for the care of mothers and children? for public health?

Local board of health, department of child welfare, county or public health nurse, extension department of state university, hospitals, local chapter American Red Cross, mental hygiene society.

8. HOW DO PEOPLE SPEND THEIR LEISURE? What facilities for recreation are there? Are they accessible to all citizens of the community? Is there sufficient variety of play opportunities for all age groups? What kinds of commercial amusement exist? Do these offer acceptable entertainment under wholesome conditions? What deficiencies and evils exist?

City park board, family welfare agency, child welfare agency, boy scouts and girl scouts organizations, community council, council of social agencies, juvenile court.

9. HOW DO YOU TAKE CARE OF PEOPLE HAVING SPECIAL NEEDS? How do you deal with people in trouble? What kinds of problems cause the greatest amount of difficulty? What welfare agencies are there to give help? Do churches and ministers work closely with social workers and welfare agencies?

Bureau of crime prevention, council of social agencies, council of churches, department of public welfare, legal aid society, Alcoholics Anonymous, probation and parole officers, public schools.

10. HOW DO MEMBERS OF MINORITY GROUPS GET ALONG? What racial, national, and cultural groups are represented? Is there discrimination or segregation in schools, hospitals, courts, places of entertainment? Are there equal opportu-

nities for housing, police protection, employment and advancement in employment? Is there evidence of tension or misunderstanding between minority and majority groups or between minorities? What opportunities exist for interracial fellowship and cooperation in community concerns? What minority groups are included in the membership, program, and outreach of your church?

Council of social agencies, labor unions, Urban League, board of education, health department, community relations board, department of public welfare, N.A.A.C.P.

11. IS THE COMMUNITY AWARE OF THE LARGER COMMUNITY? Are its citizens informed of state, national, and international developments? What response does it give to national causes and appeals? What organizations and institutions promote good citizenship, political action, and education about world affairs?

Council of churches, public library, foreign policy association or council for world affairs, labor organizations, League of Women Voters, editors of local newspapers.

12. WHO IS MEETING THE EXISTING NEEDS OF THE COMMUNITY? What are the organizations and institutions at work in the community? What churches are there, and what are they doing? In what ways do they cooperate in meeting community needs? What has your church done to serve these community needs?

Council of social agencies, council of churches, department of social welfare.[3]

Incidentally, one of the best sources of information about your community is the United States Bureau of the

---

[3] These questions and resources are adapted from *Christian Community*, Vol. 7, No. 9, November, 1955 and Vol. 8, No. 5, May, 1956. The author is indebted to the pamphlet, *Learning About Our Community* published by the Department of Social Welfare of the United Christian Missionary Society, as well as to the above named sources, for much of the material included in this compilation.

Census. Its reports tell not only how many people there are in every county and in every city of 10,000 or more (and some that are smaller), but also many significant things about them—their income, type of housing and rental value, educational level, and so on. For large cities, this information is broken down by census "tracts" or districts, so that one can get a fairly accurate picture of the immediate neighborhood in which one is most interested. Since the census is taken every ten years and several years are required to compile and publish all the data, this information may need to be supplemented by local sources of information, particularly in the latter half of the decade. Comparison of information recorded in the ten-year intervals, however, offers a good insight into trends—as well as early warning when action toward community betterment or rehabilitation may become urgent.

Go to Work

With these questions to guide you, go to work between now and the next session of this course to gather as much of the material required as possible. Pay special attention at this time to the questions grouped under Item 1, "What Is Your Community?" Perhaps its general features can be determined by looking at a map and pooling the information at the disposal of your friends or the members of your class. Fill in such related information as the following:

What is the unit you regard as your community (precinct, ward, village, town, city, county)? What is its area and population?

What is the nature of the city or area of which it is a part? What nearby cities influence the life of your community? Is it rural, village, urban, suburban?

What is its predominant economic character—industrial, commercial, agricultural? Is it an educational or recreational center? Is it primarily a residential community?

What elements in its history and tradition have affected it?

What are the physical features of the area in which your community is located? That is, is it mountainous, hilly, flat, plains?

Is your community dominated or affected by such features as rivers, ocean, large lake, canal, railroad lines, highways, air routes?

If it is farming country, what kind of soil predominates, and for what use is it best adapted?[4]

From here, you will move on to asking the other questions as to the people, their homes, their economic life, and the rest. Even if your church has a big program going on; even if there seems to be more than enough to do right now; even if you think you know the needs and the problems around you; even if you fear you don't have the resources to do anything about what you discover—take a careful look around. Consult the individuals and the agencies that have the information. Get the facts. See the whole picture as far as you can. While every commu-

---

[4] A good map of the community, showing agricultural, industrial, commercial, and residential sections in contrasting colors, could be secured or prepared and used to good advantage. Heavily populated areas could be shaded and churches located if desired.

nity is different from every other, you will find in every community people to be served, needs to be met, evils to be fought, and causes to be supported.

To get the facts, to be sure, is not an end in itself; but it is an important beginning—a necessary means to an end. You may discover new needs that ought to be met, evils that have gone unnoticed. You will be less likely to concentrate on unimportant problems while overlooking the major areas requiring attention. You will be in a better position to determine the urgent business that confronts your congregation—the big question to which all the others lead:

13. WHAT IS OUR COMMUNITY RESPONSIBILITY? In the light of the available information and the resources at our disposal, what is our obligation? What specific community ministry shall our congregation explore further and undertake now?

NOTE: In a general way, the information called for in questions 2, 3, 4, and 5 will be pertinent to the discussion of chapter 2, and questions 6, 7, 8, and 9 to chapter 3. Chapter 4 will deal with question 10 and chapter 5 with question 11 as well as many of the earlier ones. In chapter 6 the implications of the community study will be considered in the light of questions 12 and 13.

CHAPTER TWO

There Are People to Be Served

IN THE GOSPELS it is recorded that on one occasion when Jesus went ashore "he saw a great throng; and he had compassion on them." According to Matthew, he healed their sick, while according to Mark's account, "he began to teach them many things." It is not at all unlikely that he did both. Both Gospels agree that when evening came and the disciples urged him to send the crowds away so that they could buy food, Jesus replied, "You give them something to eat." The incident is one of many that illustrate the Master's interest in people and his sensitivity to the full range of their needs.

The Christian church is the legitimate heir of its Lord's deep concern for people. A church that is worthy to bear the name of Christ will share his readiness to serve them. It will not consider itself loftily superior to those physical and intellectual needs—for food, for health, for truth—which he himself was prepared to meet. If it is to minister to the whole person—and persons are whole persons or they are not persons!—the church cannot be indifferent to any valid human need.

This is not to say that the church will disregard the

so-called "spiritual" needs of the people in its community or neglect the distinctive "religious" functions of evangelism and Christian education. Men and women universally need a center of meaning for their lives, and a congregation of Christian people has an inescapable imperative to help them find that meaning in Christ and in full commitment to him. This calls for thoughtful and persistent approaches to draw persons throughout the community to such commitment and to membership in the church. If the present book does not deal at length with the evangelistic outreach of the church into its community, it is because that important outreach is the specific concern of other courses in the present series. We would, however, point out that even in its evangelistic approach to individuals, a congregation will be more effective if it has the indicated information about the people in its community and reflects in its program the total concern outlined in these pages.

There are many related personal needs, common to all, about which not very much will be said here directly. Yet awareness of these will underlie much that is said about the church's service to the community. It has long been recognized that all human beings have certain fundamental desires or psychological drives. These include the desire for love, for recognition, for self-expression, for fulfillment. To these might be added the need to give love and to render service. The church that is ministering adequately to persons will help satisfy these wants in the best way. It is not our immediate concern to suggest how the church program of worship, education, fellowship, and service helps to meet these needs. Yet here again the church that knows its community and knows its people will be in the best position to serve them.

One further word of explanation. To say that the church is interested in service to people does not mean that the church as such must necessarily administer directly all the services that are essential for good community life. Some it may well undertake directly. Others are more appropriately rendered by public or private agencies or government itself. It does mean that the church has a high trust to see that needful services are rendered and that they are available to all who need them.

The People in Your Community

Who lives here?

How many people are there?

What is the density of population, its economic, ethnic, age, sex, and educational distribution?

How long have the residents lived here?

How fast are they moving in or out?

How large are the family units?

What is the birth rate?

What are the rates of divorce and legal separation?

All of the facts indicated by these questions are important if a church is to know its community in such a manner as to serve its people. "A man's a man for a' that," but we shall have to reach him differently in a state like

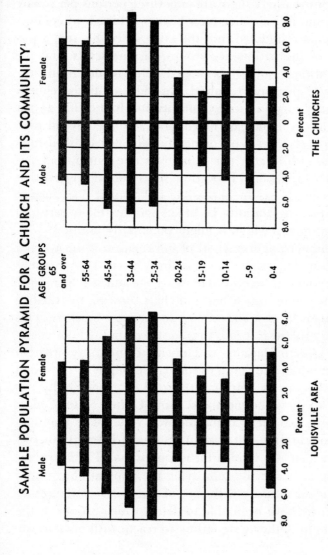

SAMPLE POPULATION PYRAMID FOR A CHURCH AND ITS COMMUNITY[1]

[1] John H. Shope, The Evangelical and Reformed Churches of Louisville, Kentucky, 1953. P. 38. Board of National Missions, Evangelical and Reformed Church.

Wyoming where there are only three persons per square mile and in a city like New York or Chicago where over 25,000 are huddled into the same space. So, too, a picture of the nationality groups, income levels, and the educational range represented helps to determine the kind of program required. An old established church recently surveyed its community and found that 25 per cent of its immediate neighbors had gone beyond high school, 48.8 per cent, or nearly half, had finished high school, while 26.2 per cent, over one-fourth, had less than a high school education. This does not mean that this church has an impossible task, but it does suggest that its program must be broad and flexible to serve all the people to whom it might potentially minister.

Another important sort of information is the age and sex distribution of the community. Some congregations have found it helpful to draw an age and sex "pyramid" of the community (that is, a chart showing the relative numbers of men and women in each age bracket). This is very useful in projecting future church school needs. One church planning to launch a community program for children and youth to combat delinquency consulted a sociologist to help it get started. Fortunately he was able to show the members, using United States Census reports, that their community was very low in the number of children but had an unusually large number of older men and women for whom no social ministry was being provided. By comparing the population pyramid of the community with that of the congregation, other churches have been able to detect which groups in the community they were failing to reach, with obvious implications alike for their pastoral, evangelistic, and social ministries.

Length of residence and degree of mobility tell us a good bit about the community and its people. Economic changes, military programs occasioned by the recent war and the current "cold" war, and the availability of transportation have made us a nation "on the move." People do not put down their roots, so that especially in cities and in new communities church work means "ministering to a procession," rather than enjoying the stable parish life of some earlier generations. This is true even in many rural areas, though in some small communities the problem is one of diminishing rather than changing population. Some students of the process assert that it is highly essential that some congregation reach the newcomer within the first three months of his arrival before he and his family develop a pattern of "getting along without the church."

The facts about family size and family disorganization almost speak for themselves. The Christian church is greatly concerned about the family. It is traditional to seek the services of a pastor when a marriage is solemnized. It is not so well established, though it is becoming recognized procedure in most churches, to seek the counsel of a pastor when difficulties trouble the family or tensions threaten its unity. Some attorneys make it their policy to refer clients seeking a divorce to a minister before accepting the case. Some courts, too, cooperate with attorneys, ministers, and social workers in a concerted effort to save marriages whenever possible. Too often, however, marriages are contracted and broken without reference to the proved resources afforded by the church.

The church's interest in the family, to be sure, goes far beyond the negative one of preventing divorce or separation, or simply holding the family together. Sometimes families separate without legal formality or stay together of necessity while unresolved tensions continue to disturb the personalities of children. The church seeks positively to provide opportunities for family participation in worship, study, service, fellowship, and other activities making for the enrichment of family life in the Christian sense.

Whoever else may be responsible for the undergirding of the families of your community, your church has a responsibility both to provide such services and to see that the community knows what services are available. It will welcome the cooperation of social agencies and all others who have the welfare of the family at heart. At the same time, the alert leadership of the congregation will be aware that its ministry to families does not stop with this direct approach. *The total well-being of every family unit and of every member of every family unit, including the units which have only one member, is involved in the kind of housing, employment, education, government, recreation, and other services the community provides.*

Thus, when we speak of serving the people of the community, we shall speak first of certain basic services all of them require and of the church's obligation to help see that they are provided. We shall then in the next chapter consider some of the special needs which emerge from peculiar individual and community circumstances. From there we shall proceed to consider some of the social evils which threaten persons and families and the causes which contribute to their fulfillment. But we shall begin with the environment factor which perhaps most immediately and directly affects the family—the house in which it lives.

The Homes in Your Community

What kinds of homes do people live in?

What percentage of the families own their own homes?

What do these homes cost?

What is the cost and condition of rental housing? Is there overcrowding? How many people per room?

Are there hotels, rooming houses, trailer camps, and other facilities which indicate transiency?

Is there need for slum clearance and low-cost housing?

Perhaps no institution in our society is so highly praised as the American home. Magazine cover pages, articles, and advertisements show it as a spacious, relatively luxurious, sunny, well painted, upper middle class suburban ranch house, equipped with every convenience, all the most recent gadgets, and a two-car garage. It is seldom mentioned that there is a heavy mortgage around the neck of the owner who has had to pay more than he could afford to provide play space for his children, the security of "nice" neighbors for his wife, and for himself the prestige of keeping up with the Joneses or staying ahead of them. Still less is there a hint that most families could not even dream of living in these lush surroundings—even though they may be buying a refrigerator (of necessity) or a television set (under pressure) or an automobile (in order once in a while to get away from it all).

The typical home "owner" has to be satisfied with a good deal less than the "House Beautiful." And great numbers of our fellow-citizens are paying exorbitant rents for space in houses that are dilapidated, obsolete, and overcrowded. In older areas of most cities one-family dwellings have been subdivided so that they "accommodate" two, four, and twelve families. Thus in Chicago between 1940 and 1950 the number of housing units without private bath or toilet increased by one half.[2] The experience of city after city has justified the statement that slum housing is most profitable for the unscrupulous landlord, and most expensive for the community. For with overcrowding come inadequate sanitary conditions, greater incidence of disease, emotional stress, delinquency, and other undesirable effects. A slum area in Denver, containing only six per cent of the population, accounted for 40 per cent of the general relief funds, 34 per cent of the aid to dependent children, 32 per cent of all police calls, and 30 per cent of the general hospital cases.[3]

A church would do well to look into its community

---

[2] *Facts About Chicago's Low-Rent Public Housing*, p. 21. Chicago Housing Authority, 1951.

[3] U. S. Municipal News, quoted in *Christian Action and Community Service*, Disciples of Christ, p. 75f.

carefully to see not only how many homes there are but also what kinds of houses they are and how many persons there are per room. Any dwelling housing more than 1.5 persons per room is seriously overcrowded; and one person per room is considered a more desirable maximum. The adequacy of the houses, the rental charges, and safety factors are all important. Nor should one assume that bad housing is uniquely the curse of the large city. A survey by the Department of Agriculture in 1945 showed that between two and one-half and three million farm houses did not meet the standard of "decent, safe, and sanitary" housing.[4] Other investigations have also indicated that rural housing lags behind urban.

The reasons behind these conditions are not far to seek. Since the first world war there have not been enough homes built to replace old worn-out housing and keep up with the growing need of a growing population. Responsible estimates are that we should build two million new homes per year for the next twenty years, in order to meet the need. But houses and apartments built by private industry have been beyond the ability of many people to buy or rent. To put it the other way, private industry has been unable (some would say, unwilling) to erect adequate housing within the reach of everyone. What then is being done to meet the problem?

1. Some groups work with local or county government officials and other community groups to see that

---

[4] *The Local Community Job Under the Housing Act of 1949*, p. 24. Housing and Home Finance Agency, 1949.

standards of occupancy, safety, and sanitation are enforced; that no illegal conversion of single-family into multiple-family units takes place; and that landlords are persuaded to cooperate with tenants and community agencies in improving property held for rental.

2. A major program, calling for federal and local cooperation, is slum clearance and public housing. Probably ten per cent, or 20,000 of the two million houses required per year, should, according to Lee F. Johnson of the National Housing Conference, be provided by low-cost public housing. Begun as a venture during the depression, this program has proved its worth both in meeting the need for housing and in helping low-income families establish themselves economically and socially. One pastor discovered that the slum area adjacent to his church which had one of the worst police records in the city came to have one of the best when it was replaced by a public housing project.

3. In some cities public assistance, in the form of public procurement of the land and certain tax concessions in return for controlled rents, has made it possible for private investors to establish moderate-cost housing. Insurance companies, labor unions, and educational institutions have recently ventured into this field.

4. Private initiative in the mass production of homes and in the organization of "planned" communities has been successful in certain instances. Generally these have served income groups somewhat above those for whom government housing is needed.

5. A few experiments in cooperative housing have been undertaken. The purpose is to take advantage of

the economies of multiple-unit building, while permitting the member to have an equity in his unit. The cooperative exercises certain controls over resale and makes for good community living.

6. Federally guaranteed mortgages (FHA) have been of help in making bank loans available to more would-be home buyers. In addition, special concessions have been given war veterans in consideration of their service to the nation.

All of these developments indicate an awareness of the problem on the part of forward-looking leaders in government, business, and labor. But it takes everlasting effort to keep before local officials, national lawmakers, and an indifferent public the stake that each of us has in seeing that there is adequate shelter for all. The church has a unique responsibility to act as a conscience to see that people, especially the "least" and "downmost," find housing, and decent housing at that.

Economic Needs

What is the economic character of the community?

What is the income range of the people?

How do they make their living?

What problems do they face in their daily work?

What is the relation between labor and management, businessman and consumer, farmer and townsman?

Is any economic group insufficiently represented in the leadership of the churches?

The Christian faith takes a very sane and wholesome view of the economic problem. The same Lord who quoted the Scripture, "Man does not live by bread alone," taught his disciples to pray, "Give us this day our daily bread." When the Christian Church is faithful to his direction, it recognizes that the economic and material aspect of life is not *sufficient*, but highly *important*. And the "spiritual values" of which one hears so much relate to the way in which we deal with such mundane affairs as money, jobs, food, and clothes.

Some of the information called for in the above battery of questions will be considered in subsequent chapters. For the moment we are concerned primarily with asking whether the basic economic needs of everyone in the community are taken care of, and how well. A comparison of actual income range with estimated average "health and decency" budgets will suggest individuals and groups whose living is not sufficient or secure, for whom something more than the "iron law of wages" or an irresponsible reliance on "supply and demand" must be provided.

The National Study Conference on the Church and Economic Life, convened by the National Council of Churches in Pittsburgh in 1956, addressed itself to the problem of "The Christian Conscience and an Economy of Abundance." One section of the Conference Message called attention to the ironical situation which still prevails in rich America:

> We must recognize the fact that even as we complain of "surplus" there are in our own country large numbers of people who do not share in the general abundance. Im-

proved as is the distribution of income in our country and profoundly encouraging as is the substantial increase in the welfare and income of the middle groups in the economic scale, it is still true that about one-fourth of all families in the United States have annual incomes of less than $2,000, not nearly enough to sustain a life of health and hope. Among those whose share in the general abundance is particularly low are most of the smaller scale farm families, some groups of wage-earners, and numbers of recent immigrants and newcomers to our country. Moreover, discrimination and segregation practices against minority races deprive many of their members of the chance to earn a fair share of the fruits of the new age or to contribute in their full measure to the nation's welfare. The Christian conscience in an age of abundance must be troubled until these pockets of want are changed to areas of opportunity."[5]

Take a good look at your community to see how the following get along income-wise—migrants, day laborers, domestic servants, immigrants, minority group persons, widows with dependent children. What are the reasons for low income: inadequate laws, unscrupulous employers, regional or local economic decline, shifting industry? What can be done to serve the victims?

The Schools in Your Community

What are the schools like?

What sort of educational facilities are provided?

What standards prevail? What are the chief needs or problems of the schools?

---

[5] *American Abundance,* Message of the Third National Study Conference on the Church and Economic Life, p. 8f. National Council of the Churches of Christ in the U.S.A., 1956.

Are equal privileges open to all children of the community without discrimination?

What opportunities for education are offered to adults and young people after they leave school?

Not least among the people to be served in every normal community are the children. Apart from a good family, a satisfactory home, basic economic security, and the church itself, no service that society renders for its children is more essential than education. The school is in a sense the daughter of the church, and American Protestantism has been deeply interested in the cause of free public education.

If your church is concerned for the future of your community, it will keep an eye open to the best interests of the public school. Individuals or groups desiring a more complete guide for evaluating the local school system can find 150 questions in chapter 7 of Roland L. Warren's *Studying Your Community,* to which reference was made earlier. Various educational associations also have produced standards, and a number of books have been written on the subject.

Perhaps a few comments to supplement the brief "lead" questions printed above will indicate major problems one may expect to find:

1. School authorities have for some time been pointing up the nationwide need for additional buildings and classrooms to take care of replacing obsolete equipment and meet the growing public school population which is expected to exceed 37 million by 1960 as compared with 30 million in elementary and secondary

schools in 1955. With a current shortage of 250,000 classrooms, estimates of construction needs run as high as 950,000 additional classrooms by 1965 with costs ranging between 15 and 30 billion dollars. Various proposals for apportioning the cost between local, state, and federal authorities have been considered. The principle of local responsibility is acknowledged by all, but some federal assistance is required because not all sections of the country are equally able to provide sufficient funds to give their children schooling comparable to the best or even the average within the nation. In many instances, however, schools look to community-minded citizens to take the lead in promoting tax levies and bond issues for needed buildings.

2. The teacher shortage is equally serious. It is estimated that 135,000 teachers are needed right now to replace retiring and inadequately trained teachers. Perhaps 20,000 additional teachers are required to care for a school population growing at the rate of 1,500,000 per year. Church people can help the schools by seeing that teachers are adequately paid, that young people learn to regard teaching as a Christian vocation, and that there are no barriers to the employment of competent teachers belonging to racial and cultural minorities.

3. The quality of the teaching program is an important matter for citizen concern. While many "cranks" belabor the schools for allegedly introducing "fads and frills," it is more valuable to ask whether tested improvements in curriculum and teaching methods have been adopted and how adequate preparation for vocation or higher education is.

4. A special concern for the churches is that the schools be kept free from outside pressures that interfere with the unbiased examination of all points of view, including those which find fewest supporters in the community. It is, for example, ridiculous to suppose that young people can effectively withstand the appeal of subtly presented philosophies such as communism and atheism, if they do not have opportunity to examine and discuss them.

5. Because it is just, because it is the law of the land, and because it is best for both majority and minority group children, church people should work with school authorities and citizens' groups to eliminate any remaining traces of racial segregation.

6. The public school should not become the pawn of any religious pressure group, Protestant, Jewish, Roman Catholic, or secularistic. However, we should work with citizens of all faiths to encourage the schools to study objectively and fairly the place of religion in society ancient and modern, and the significance of various religious traditions, including their own, as such material is pertinent to their courses in history, literature, music, art, and modern problems.

For further information on the relation of the church to the school, consult the Department of Religion and Public Education of the National Council of Churches, 257 Fourth Avenue, New York 10, New York.

These Churches Took Action

CASE A. The Euclid Avenue Congregational Church in Cleveland, Ohio, is an old established congregation,

on a formerly fashionable thoroughfare now given over
largely to business establishments. Its older members
have moved to the suburbs, and the side streets off of
Euclid Avenue now house humbler families. Trained
visitors interviewed 1696 households, or 58 per cent of
the 2920 in the area immediately surrounding the
church. The remaining 42 per cent represented vacancy,
absence from home, or refusal of information. Only 39
families in the area belonged to Euclid Avenue Church,
1009 reported other church affiliation or interest, and
648 were considered prospects for further visitation, 179
of them expressing a desire for further contact. Of the
3533 individuals belonging to the households interviewed, 3119 (88.2 per cent) were white, 372 (10.6 per
cent) were Negro, and 42 (1.2 per cent) belonged to
other racial groups. Of the persons giving information,
27.9 per cent had been in the community less than one
year, 40.6 per cent between 1 and 5 years, and 31.5 per
cent over 5 years. Significant data about the age distribution of its neighbors were also gathered. As a result
of this survey the congregation has under consideration
a number of suggestions for a more effective ministry to
its immediate community. Fact-finding thus becomes
the basis of improved program. (Data from *Report of
Community Religious Survey,* Euclid Avenue Congregational Church, February-March, 1956.)

CASE B. The Church of Christ on Oak Street in New
Haven, Connecticut, carried on a campaign to get rid
of rats in its community, got signatures petitioning the
city government for a housing code, and operated a
weekend work-camp to paint and repair people's houses.

(*The Friend,* reported in Ross W. Sanderson's *The Church Serves the Changing City,* p. 187.)

CASE C. The Congregational Christian churches of Chicago became concerned with the city's need of new public housing. Federal funds were available, but the chief difficulty was the unwillingness of most communities to accept new housing projects to house the people who would be moved out of the areas where further projects would be built. A group of laymen made possible the preparation of a filmstrip to be shown in the churches, demonstrating the moral and economic scandal of the city's slums and the prejudice against public housing projects.

CASE D. Memorial Protestant Episcopal Church in Baltimore, Maryland, is one of a growing number of churches working with social agencies and city planning groups for urban redevelopment. Among other interests, it is working for a new school, new playgrounds, and better housing. It gives financial help to selected institutions and has placed its parish house at the disposal of various community groups. (*The Parish: Power House of Your Community,* National Council of the Protestant Episcopal Church.)

CASE E. A labor union, turned down in its demand for improved working conditions, a slight wage increase, and a contract, called a strike against a textile mill in an industrial section of Cleveland, Ohio. The management used the strike as an excuse for liquidating the company. Both Protestant and Roman Catholic clergymen joined with other civic leaders in appealing for reconsideration or at least opportunity to secure a purchaser who would save the business and the employees' jobs. The union withdrew its wage demands, but the stockholders accepted the decision of the management to liquidate. (Reported in *Christian Community*.)

CASE F. Several years ago, a community in eastern Pennsylvania was bitterly debating the proposed consolidation of two school districts. The "pro's" held meetings and told their story. The "anti's" held meetings and denounced the "pro's." The social action committee of Salem Evangelical and Reformed Church in Catasauqua decided to hold a public meeting in which each side could tell its story, listen to the other, and submit to questions from the audience. It was reported that this was the one opportunity many citizens had to hear the whole story and make up their minds.

CASE G. During the second world war, Chicago's First Baptist Church called the Rev. Jitsuo Morikawa, an American of Japanese descent, as its associate pastor, and began a ministry to Japanese Americans who were then moving from the relocation centers to the city. Later, when the senior pastor resigned, Dr. Morikawa was called to that office, and the congregation ministered to Negroes as well. The membership of Caucasians as well as of others has shown steady increase. The church cooperated with local and national Baptist agencies and with the Hyde Park YMCA in establishing a community center. Its educational and recreational facilities are made available on weekday afternoons and evenings to meet the needs of a religiously and socially heterogeneous population, through the services of a director, three part-time assistants, and 35 volunteers. The Christian motivation, Christian worship, and Christian educational programs remain central; and an impressive increase in giving has been experienced.

What do you think of the above cases? Could your group try something along the same line so that the people in your community may be better served?

CHAPTER THREE

There Are Needs to Be Met

THE CONGREGATION that places its accent on people will be alert to see that their needs are met. As it studies its community it will begin to discover many needs. Some of these are quite general needs which affect everyone directly and call for concerted citizen effort which may be readily forthcoming. Such might be the need for better schools or good government. On the other hand, there will be some relatively specialized requirements affecting a limited section of the population for whom provision must be made either for the protection of the entire community or on the grounds of human and neighborly concern. Thus low-cost public housing, as we have seen, may be the answer to the acute need of families having insufficient income but may also contribute materially to the reduction of disease, crime, and friction in the community as a whole. So, too, tuberculosis and mental illness represent specific problems calling for cooperative community action.

In the preceding chapter we have called attention to some of the basic services which are required in every community—housing, employment, and education—

and to examples of action taken by churches and church groups toward their improvement. In this chapter we shall similarly deal with some further needs of people, for which provision must be made as a survey in any given parish may indicate. For more exhaustive treatment of these problems the reader is referred to the guides suggested on page 11 and in the bibliography at the end of the text. But it is our hope that this present inquiry may serve as a beginning for a long-term process of study, service, and action in your church's wider ministry.

Good Government

How is the community governed?

What is the status of law enforcement and the administration of justice?

What are the facts about crime and delinquency?

What provision is made for the treatment and rehabilitation of offenders?

What measures are taken, or needed, to prevent delinquency?

How fully do citizens participate in the processes of government?

Are civil liberties adequately protected?

From the days of the New Testament, Christians have been of two minds about government. On the one hand, there is the teaching of Paul that "the powers that be are ordained of God," that civil authority is instituted to restrain the evil conduct of sinful men, to establish order, and to promote the common good. On the other hand, the early Christians were soon aware that it is possible for the state to overreach its authority, to use its power unjustly, and to claim for Caesar what belongs to God alone.

Some present-day Christians are afraid of government. Some are content to permit the processes of government to operate without regard to their purposes and convictions as Christians and to make something of a virtue out of "keeping religion and politics apart." If, however, we take seriously both aspects of the historic Christian view, we shall use government gratefully as one of the established channels for the service of God and man, and at the same time keep its policies and its workings under the critical judgment of the Christian conscience.

At the very minimum Christians must recognize the *necessity* of government as the precondition of any kind of secure and stable community life, and the *importance* of government because it affects everyone within the community.

In our complex world with its multiplying needs and problems, it is inevitable that government and public agencies should play a larger role than ever. It is therefore essential that church people understand how their community is governed, how its laws are written, who administers them and how.

Nor is this interest confined to the negative or critical function of denouncing dishonest and lawless officials. We shall say more about dealing with such overt evils in chapter 4. Corruption and favoritism and "boss" rule are bad and must be fought. However, good government in the second half of the twentieth century means far more than the absence of graft and collusion with law-breaking elements. It means having a modern and effective structure of government, generally prescribed in a charter drawn up by a representative and able group of citizens and approved by a public election. It means placing clearly defined responsibility for basic policy decisions in "visible" elected and appointed officials, with a merit system covering employees responsible for carrying out these policies and the day-to-day routine operations of the government unit. It means sound and wise administration of the many services a county, township, or city has a right to expect of its officials. It means seeing to it that provision is made for new services as they are required, and for eliminating what is no longer needed. And it means making sure that the services offered are available to everyone regardless of race, economic status, or geographical district.

An important aspect of community government, too, is the courts. It is not only in certain large cities but often, too, in rural counties that the lower courts especially are allowed to degenerate because of the apathy of citizens who ought to have the public interest at heart. Able and fair men and women should be encouraged to run for such posts or to accept appointment to them, and the community should pay adequate salaries to enable them to do so. Policemen and police officials, too, should be paid enough to attract competent personnel, and should be held to the faithful discharge of their duty. It should be understood that this means not only persistence in the apprehension of violators of the law but also a scrupulous regard for civil rights and legal processes in handling suspected or proven violators.

There is an aspect of community life which we commonly overlook when we think of government. That is the "power structure" of the community. True enough, this is not an official part of the governing process, yet it is very real. In every community, as well as in the state and the nation as a whole, there are individuals and groups whose influence is much greater than the combined power of many others. In one city, for example, it is said that four banks determine in what neighborhoods Negroes may buy homes. Some states are known to be under the control of mining or gambling or dairying or cotton "interests." And many national issues are determined by the interplay of such forces as "big business," "organized labor," and the "farm bloc."

At the very least, we must recognize and identify the groups that exercise power in our community if we are going to secure or preserve good government—the owners of the largest industries, the publishers of the leading newspapers, the lending institutions and real estate boards, the county "bosses," and the like. In many instances we may be able to win their support for a desired end. In some cases it may be wise to work with some of these forces against the objectives of others. Sometimes it is necessary to oppose one or another of them directly.

While some of these groups have little respect for the churches and other "do-gooders," many of them spend a considerable amount of time and effort to cultivate the good will of organizations like the church, which possess a certain amount of respectability and prestige. For if prestige without power is at times ineffective, power without prestige can be very embarrassing. If this situation can be exploited without compromise of principle, some conflicts can be mitigated and social gains registered which would otherwise have a much longer and more doubtful history.

If good government is a basic need of every community, who has a deeper interest in securing it than the people who make up the church of Christ? This does not mean that they should make the church as an institution the instrument of any given candidate, party, or cause. Neither does it mean that any one church should control the choice of officials or dictate the policies of the government. It does place upon Christian people the responsibility of exerting their influence wisely in the selection of candidates and the formulation of public policy. Such influence must begin long before election time in the councils and caucuses of political parties and citizens' movements, and it must be exerted continuously when laws or policy decisions affecting the common welfare are being formulated.

Much of our Christian influence will necessarily be exerted through the responsible action of Christians. But the church itself has the obligation to see that its members know their duty as Christians, become familiar with candidates and issues, have opportunity to hear the presentation of the major problems and to participate in the discussion of them, formulate their corporate judgment on selected questions in which important principles are at stake, and receive guidance as to the strategic time and method of action.

Good Health

What is the state of the community's health?

Who gets sick, and why?

What are the birth and death rates per thousand?

What provision is made for treating contagious disease? for improving mental health? for the care of mothers and children? for public health?

What problems are associated with the sale and use of alcoholic beverages?

Probably nothing more vividly dramatizes the contrast between the Christian religion and many of its rivals in the Orient than the attitude toward human health and life. In many eastern lands the traditional expression in the presence of disease was, "It is the will of God." Into these areas came Christian missionaries building hospitals, leprosaria, and clinics, proclaiming a Savior who brings health and sanity for the whole person.

We often think of illness as an individual problem calling for purely individual treatment. The individual patient, to be sure, remains the object of our solicitude and our efforts at relief and cure. And we rightly value the personal ministry of physician and nurse who prescribe and administer medication. However, behind them is a great complex of research and experimentation, the pooling of specialized information, and the activity of public agencies which establish standards of sanitation and protect the community from contagious disease.

"Who gets sick, and why," and "Who dies from what" become very significant questions for your community. Scientific and technical advances have done much to reduce the danger of many of the once deadly communicable diseases, but the so-called chronic diseases make a correspondingly more serious impact as the average life span increases. Perhaps even more important from the standpoint of what church people and other citizens can do, the mere advance of science does not of itself guarantee that everyone will benefit equally. There are still congested districts of the city and "pockets of want" among the poorer families in both town and country, where cost tends to put first class medical care and the preventive and curative "miracle drugs" out of reach. The community-conscious church will be alert to call attention to areas or groups which may be getting less than an equal chance at good health services. If there is need of additional county nurses, public health department personnel, school health programs, clinics for mothers and children, or counsel on family planning, this would not be the first time that the church initiated such a movement.

Then, too, there are special kinds of health needs to which the church should be sensitive, especially if no one else appears to care about them. One of these is *mental illness.* Many of those to whom our Lord brought healing during his earthly ministry were "tormented by demons" or, as we should say, emotionally ill. For a long time we made only small progress in meeting this need, because those so afflicted lacked influence or spokesmen and those related by blood or marriage were helpless or ashamed in the presence of the problem. A more wholesome attitude has brought about a greater readiness to discuss the need objectively; but, even so, much needs to be done. Many people still fail to understand that there are varieties of mental disorder requiring quite varied treatment, and that many patients if treated early enough have an excellent chance of recovery. Frequently, too, there is a reluctance on the part of state legislators to provide adequately for this group who have neither a vote nor a lobby. Yet mental illness accounts for more illness than any other except the arthritic diseases; and mental health patients occupy over half of all hospital beds.[1] Increased longevity, the growing pressure of our high-speed life, and better methods of detecting incipient nervous disabilities combine to make the need for therapy more acute than ever.

The other special problem is *alcoholism*. There may be some who would question whether this is strictly speaking a health problem. It will be readily agreed that normally up to a certain point which varies with the individual, the use or excessive use of beverage alcohol is within the realm of a person's control, and it is his moral responsibility to avoid such use as demonstrably slows his responses, clouds his judgment, and releases his inhibitions. However, it is equally clear that the "problem drinker" at some point develops a dependence on alcohol and loses his capacity to control his choice, un-

---

[1] Katherine Glover, *Mental Health; Everybody's Business,* p. 4. Public Affairs Pamphlet No. 196.

til in the alcoholic one sees a man who is as truly sick as the paranoid, though in a different way, and requires competent therapy. In such therapy he must cooperate; yet the nature of his illness is such that he must admit that he cannot master it alone; he must seek and accept help. Alcoholics Anonymous has successfully applied this truth which is grounded in the insights of Christian faith. The church, concerned as it is both for the victim himself and for the welfare of his family, will welcome such resources as "AA" and psychiatry. At the same time it recognizes in this person one whom the Great Physician would heal—not so much by belaboring the man for his vile behavior as by offering him the peace of God, a meaning and fulfillment for his life which makes unnecessary and uninteresting the false escape on which he has come to depend.

The problem of health brings together in a most revealing manner the variety of resources which the community has to offer. The individual's own material resources have had to be supplemented by private hospitalization insurance funds—and there *may* come a time when health insurance like social security will be handled by government. We have referred to physicians and surgeons in private practice and on public health services. We recognize the importance of hospitals, some administered by churches, some by private associations, some by county, city, or state. We must add, too, the various voluntary health organizations set up in the interest of specialized problems—cancer, cerebral palsy, and so on. There are said to be more than 20,000 of these in the United States alone. Just as the church pioneered in founding hospitals, it may today make a contribution through discovering and meeting new needs or encouraging the community through private and public agencies to meet them.

Recreation and Leisure Time

How do people spend their leisure?

What facilities for recreation are there? Are they accessible to all citizens of the community? Is there sufficient variety of play opportunities for all age groups?

What kinds of commercial amusement exist? Do these offer acceptable entertainment under wholesome conditions?

What deficiencies and evils exist?

Closely related to man's need for health is his need for good, wholesome recreation. If the church has sometimes taken a dim view of "worldly pleasure," it may have been in part because the exponents of sport have overdone it or because some forms of leisure-time activity had unsavory associations which raised moral questions for sensitive Christians. Nevertheless, there have been Christian groups who frowned on play as a frivolous and wicked activity in a world where there were more important things to do. This view, however, does not reflect the considered judgment of responsible present-day Christians who believe that neither the ascetic nor the "play-boy" has found the way.

Today there is little danger that recreation will be

under-emphasized. We have a multi-billion dollar entertainment industry, with spectator sports, hobbies, television, theater, motion picture, and participant sports vying with each other for the leisure time the individual is expected to have as a result of the shortened work week and labor-saving devices.

Nor is there any likelihood that any great part of the Christian church will denounce recreational activity as in itself sinful. We are too much aware of the need of man for relief from his labor—a respite that was built into the Hebrew consciousness by the institution of the Sabbath and rescued from legalistic distortion by Christ himself.

However, the question is very much in order whether —with all our professional football games, drive-in theaters, bowling leagues, and life-or-death bridge games— we are using, or offering, adequate *recreational* opportunities. There is a difference between recreation and amusement, between leisure-time activities that place a premium upon personal participation, mental stimulation, family and inter-personal fellowship, and personal growth, and those which offer passive spectacles or second-hand excitement. So if we are judging how well the need for recreation is being met, we do not count the number of theaters and measure the size of the stadium. We do better to look at how well playgrounds and parks are distributed in relation to population, what kinds of programs and facilities are available to everyone, and how well they are used.

The church itself may, of course, offer good leisure-time resources. In addition to its regular education and service programs, many a church has offered a home to groups looking for fellowship and activity opportunities —boy scouts, teenage clubs, golden-agers, and others. But this does not exhaust its responsibility, for the total provision of the total community may depend on the word and influence of a group that takes it upon itself to speak and work for the whole need of the whole man wherever he is.

Other Special Needs

How do you take care of people having special needs?

How do you deal with people in trouble?

What kinds of problems cause the greatest amount of difficulty?

What welfare agencies are there to give help?

Do churches and ministers work closely with social workers and welfare agencies?

In addition to the rather broadly defined needs arising out of the general characteristics of man in society, there are many special needs growing out of the make-up, experience, or status of the individual. One measure of the maturity of the community is how well it recognizes these needs and seeks to meet them. And one measure of the sensitivity of a local church is its response to the special needs manifested among the people within and about the life of its own parish.

Many churches have found it helpful to use a check-list against which they can begin to look for groups and individuals who in a peculiar way need help. Such a list,

embodying some of the kinds of needs we have already
discussed, might include the following:

—Adults
—Aging
—Alcoholic
—Children
—Chronic invalids
—Delinquents or
  pre-delinquents
—Displaced persons
—Divided families
—Handicapped
—Homeless men
—Immigrants or foreign lan-
  guage groups (list them)
—Migrant workers and
  families
—Night workers
—Orphans
—Parents
—Paroled prisoners
—Racial minorities
  (list them)
—Striking workers
—Teenagers
—Tenant farmers
—Transients
—Underprivileged
—Unemployed
—Unmarried adults
—Working mothers
—Young adults

In many communities, the needs of the *aging* are
coming very much to the fore. Surely here is an opportunity to make life meaningful for people who need fellowship and a sense that they are needed. Here is also
a resource that may be utilized, skill and experience
that may be placed in the service of the church.

Earlier in the scale of age are the *youth* of church and
community with their special needs. What facilities for
fellowship, recreation, and wise, friendly counsel are offered youth who might become, or may already be, de-
linquent?

And, in between, is anyone taking an interest in *other
people who may be in trouble*—prisoners on parole, for
instance? In one rural county (and there are hundreds
like it) a well informed person stated that it was virtual-

ly impossible to get men to sponsor young prisoners eligible for parole (in many instances first-time offenders who might be saved from further trouble). In one large city (and it might have been many another) juvenile court officials were distressed that there was no Protestant agency to whose care adolescent girls might be assigned for assistance when involved in difficulties.

Another group requiring special kinds of service are the *handicapped*. Some individuals whose handicaps may be obvious often awaken a kind of sympathy and sometimes come to depend on charity. In some cities the Goodwill Industries offer such persons an opportunity to work. But far more opportunities need to be created in normal industrial and commercial situations, adjusted perhaps to take account of the individual's special skills and difficulties.

Some groups are marked because they do not seem to "belong." In many rural communities migrant workers are regarded as outcasts, not even welcome in a Christian church. In other areas church people and community leaders have tried to make up for the advantages and services such "transients" usually miss. Recent immigrants are sometimes "frozen" out, and race discrimination is a common evil. On the other hand, the sponsoring of displaced persons has been a thrilling and beneficent experience in many a congregation.

All around there are people to be served and needs to be met. When a congregation takes a serious look at its community in the light of its own nature and calling as the creature and servant of Christ, it is certain to find them—and to find ways of meeting these needs. It may be in the church program itself: Is there need for a worship service at some time other than Sunday morning at eleven for certain workers? Do working mothers or business and professional women get left out of church life because all the women's activities are in the afternoon? What must be done to make an effective evangelistic appeal to the intellectual, the Puerto Rican, the stranger in the community? Or the task may call for the stimulation of community resources.

In any event the church must heed the need and consider how it should be met. For there is in our Bible a parable of a great Day when the King will pronounce this terrible judgment: "I was hungry and you gave me no food, I was thirsty and you gave me no drink, I was a stranger and you did not welcome me, naked and you did not clothe me, sick and in prison and you did not visit me." And when the accused protest that there must be some mistake, the explanation is quite evident: they had been in the presence of need and had done nothing to meet it; and as they failed their brethren they had failed their Lord.

These Churches Took Action

CASE A. The men's group of a church in a county seat town checked the registration lists and telephoned a reminder to every member of the church who had not registered for the coming election.

CASE B. When a Citizen's Commission was formed to study the governmental structure of a large metropolitan county, it invited various industrial, labor, and other organizations to appoint representatives. The Council of Churches was not among the groups invited, but when its officers made known the interest of the churches in better government, it was urged to appoint a representative also.

CASE C. In Big Lick, Tennessee, in the Cumberland Mountains, the church under the dynamic leadership of Pastor Eugene Smathers has been instrumental in organizing a Farmers' Association through which expensive farm machinery could be purchased and used cooperatively; a health center with a nurse who not only conducts a clinic but visits in the homes of the area; and a loan fund to enable young men to begin farming on reasonable terms.

CASE D. Gethsemane Protestant Episcopal Church, in downtown Minneapolis, ministers to transients in nearby hotels, but reaches into the blighted area nearby to offer a program for children having no supervision or play opportunities after school. One of its two curates works with probation officers, juvenile judges, and other courts; the other serves the public hospitals. In addition, the director of the interdenominational committee on work with American Indians in the Twin City area has his office in the parish house. (From *The Parish: Power House of Your Community*.)

CASE E. During the second world war the mental hospitals of the state of Iowa suffered seriously for lack of personnel. A number of conscientious objectors were assigned to work in these institutions under the Civilian Public Service program authorized by the Selective Service Act. It was discovered that standards of care were low, and that the interest of the people of the state was, to judge by appropriations, even lower. A group of concerned church people, pastors, laymen, and women of various denominations, together with other civic-minded persons, formed a co-ordinating committee. As a result of a statewide educational campaign, the entire mental hospital program of the state was put on a more adequate foundation.

CASE F. The Heights Christian Church, in an elite suburb of Cleveland, became interested in the work of the Cleveland Mental Health Association. As a result it displayed and distributed materials dealing with mental health. It next challenged the businessmen of the community to cooperate in maintaining and improving the character of the suburb's shopping district. Next, following the example of the pastor and his wife, a number of families offered temporary foster home care for the children's service agency. Members of the church cooperate with the Community Fund, serve as nurses' aides in the hospitals, and bring residents of the county home for the aged to the church for dinner, worship, and fellowship.

CASE G. In Youngstown, Ohio, the Lutheran Service Society, supported by members of many Lutheran churches in Northeastern Ohio, operates a Day Center for Senior Citizens. Three days a week the first floor rooms below the Society's offices are open for reading, games, singing, hobby shows, or informal educational and recreational programs. One unusual activity sponsored with the assistance of the Kiwanis Club is a Senior Citizens' Camp, held for one week during the summer.

CASE H. The Judson Memorial Church, in New York's

Greenwich Village, several years ago began work with a gang of boys who had a reputation for purse snatching, car stealing, and going from settlement house to settlement house creating trouble. The effort was made to work very patiently with this group without resort to punishment. There were a number of disappointing and destructive experiences. However, after securing the release of some of the gang leaders from the police, the Center became the haven for "the rejects from every social agency in Lower Manhattan." There have followed interest projects, counseling, and work with courts, probation officers, and detention homes. (From an article in *The City Church*.)

CASE I. Fourteen Evangelical and Reformed churches in an area extending some thirty-four miles along the Ohio River several years ago became aware that both the economic condition and the spiritual vitality of the area were declining. Many farms were being abandoned, and churches were being closed. Strip-mining and erosion had contributed to the forlorn appearance of the terrain. The ministers and lay leaders of these churches were instrumental in organizing a soil conservation district and in cooperating with the state agricultural extension service. There has resulted better use of land, with improved crops, poultry, and cattle. These congregations have banded together as the Pioneer Larger Parish. The pastors, while having primary responsibility for their own congregations, work together on many common problems as a team under the direction of the parish council. A rural church pilgrimage, in which this group cooperated with other denominations, resulted in the formation of a County Planning Committee, with subcommittees on industrial development, public health, schools, and welfare. Thus the churches of a dying rural community have gained a head start in meeting the problems and opportunities arising from a $350,000,000 industrial development program scheduled for this area.

CHAPTER FOUR

There Are Evils to Be Corrected

As A CHRISTIAN takes a thoughtful look around his community, he is certain to find some conditions which outrage his conscience. If he is fully pleased with everything he sees, one may conclude either that he has not really seen what is there or that his conscience has become so well conformed to his little world as to have lost the essential capacity to measure things by the perfect standard of the mind of Christ. No earthly community is such a Utopia that there are not in it evils that cry out for correction. Though some neighborhoods may have fewer serious problems than others, it is unlikely that any Christian group that has proceeded thus far in checking up on the homes, the government, the economic life, and the other institutions in its vicinity will have failed to find some situation which compels one to say, "Here is something more than a lack which must be supplied; here is an evil we must combat."

Crime and Corruption

How is the community governed?

What is the status of law enforcement and the administration of justice?

What are the facts about crime and delinquency?

Are civil rights and civil liberties adequately protected?

The first place to which the concerned citizen commonly turns to judge the seriousness of the plight of a city, township, or county is its record for law observance and law enforcement. Whether there is crime, the amount and kind of crime, the record on apprehension of criminals, the safety and security of persons, the enforcement of regulations affecting the health and welfare of citizens, and especially the trend, for better or worse, over a five or ten year period—all of these facts are important if we are to avoid the futile extremes of complacency and hysteria.

Recent investigations like that of the Kefauver Committee have reminded us of the extent of organized crime and the tie-up which sometimes exists between such criminal groups and local governments. They also remind us that such connections are not confined to gangs that specialize in extortion, robbery, and murder; they cover not only gambling syndicates but also groups engaged in legitimate business which use personal "influence" or bribery to secure contracts and special privileges from government. At the same time we must remember that, however serious these revelations are, there are many incorruptible officials attempting to administer their trust effectively. Indeed, studies like that of the United States Senate Subcommittee on Ethical Standards in Government indicate that the standards prevailing in the national government are at a higher level than those observed in much of the world of private business.

How a church goes about dealing with lawlessness depends, of course, upon the precise problem it faces. If taverns in the neighborhood sell liquor to minors, or violate the regulations covering closing hours, this is a simple matter of asking local police officials to enforce the law. Similarly in the case of gambling, prostitution, and the sale of narcotics, the vigilance of citizens cooperating with churches, schools, and social agencies, is the best stimulus to police action. Enforcement of housing codes calls for even more effective community organization if deterioration and blight are to be prevented, for most cities have inadequate staffs for inspection, and the police are generally occupied with minute-to-minute emergencies and crimes of violence.

As a rule, citizens are well advised not to attempt to do the work of the police for them! They will rather cooperate, and assume a readiness to cooperate, in the interest of law and order and public safety. In certain situations citizens' groups have taken the initiative in getting evidence against violators, but ordinarily this is best left to trained professionals. In those cases where there is collusion between city officials or police officers and criminals, citizens may have to appeal to higher government units—state or federal—or organize politically to replace the group that is misusing its power. In such a case, needless to say, it is preferable that representative church people of various denominations and of all faiths, *both clergy and lay,* participate in the effort

rather than that a church as such be identified as supporting certain candidates. On the *issues* the church has
a right and a duty to speak. Its leaders and representatives have the right and duty to take active part in this,
as in any, political movement. One should, however,
beware of giving the absolute sanction of the church to
our relative, imperfect political alternatives.

One danger when Christians become involved in politics is that their concern will be manifested on too narrow a front. We may see the damage done by organized
gambling or a predatory alcoholic beverage industry. At
the same time we may not be sufficiently sensitive to in-
terference with civil liberties. For example, in some
communities irresponsible organizations have brought
pressure upon public libraries not to purchase, display,
or circulate books displeasing to these groups. Various
devices have been used to prevent the organization of
labor unions. Police have used brutality on prisoners in
custody. Some local courts have permitted such abuses
to go on. At times, too, the moral zeal of crusading citizens will make them insufficiently sensitive to the civil
and human rights of persons suspected of criminal behavior, who are presumed innocent unless proven guilty
and who even if guilty are entitled to a fair trial!

Another danger to which we are subject is that we
will be superficial in our diagnosis and therefore inadequate in our approach to a cure. It is to be expected
that law-abiding citizens, such as church members are
likely to be, will readily grasp the importance of enforcing the laws that have to do with the protection of
life and property, and will be interested in seeing that

"something is done about crime and delinquency." They may not, however, see that this involves taking constructive measures to prevent delinquency as well as efforts to "crack down" on offenders, or that additional probation officers may be even more necessary than additional patrolmen. One of the poorest examples of good citizenship is the occasional civic group or "improvement" association which demands a war on crime while its members call for lower taxes and vote down bond issues for better schools, housing, playgrounds, welfare services, and street lighting. The deacon who complains that "the boys in this neighborhood are making a nuisance of themselves," might ask: "What can our church do to offer them constructive activity and guidance?"

Exploitation

What is the income range of the people? How do they make their living?

How do people spend their leisure? What kinds of commercial amusement exist? Do these offer acceptable entertainment under wholesome conditions? What deficiencies and evils exist?

What problems are associated with the sale and use of alcoholic beverages?

Many of the grosser evils which beset the community have been outlawed as crimes and thus have the force of government as well as public opinion aligned against them. But there are other sinister forces, only partly or inadequately subject to the control of law, which can be held in check only as civic conscience, public opinion, or organized pressure are brought to bear upon them. In some instances moral disapproval based on good publicity are sufficient to check the danger. In other cases aroused civic concern may have to press for new controls or sanctions which may take the form of new laws promoting the common welfare. The problem of evil "inside the law" can be illustrated by various organized interests, generally having economic motives and ends, that exploit the needs and wants of people, whether for beauty, wealth, or comfort.

A common phenomenon in our society is gambling in its various forms. Some of these manifestations, particularly commercially organized gambling in which the "take" runs into fantastic figures, are problems for police and court action under existing laws. The bookmakers, "policy" and "numbers" racketeers, and slot-machine magnates are a constant menace to good community life and honest law enforcement. Sometimes these professionals attempt to use charitable organizations or even church groups as respectable pawns for their purposes. In many states, too, there is agitation to make gambling legal.

Even when it is divorced from criminal auspices, gambling makes financial and psychological slaves of many people on every social level. Church groups can perhaps meet this aspect of the problem most effectively by educating their youth as to the effects of gambling, by encouraging more creative types of recreation, and by scrupulously avoiding activities which involve or border on gambling.

One of the particularly sordid developments of recent years, which has occasioned considerable comment and controversy, is the production of so-called "comic" books depicting crime, horror, and distorted values, for sale to impressionable boys and girls in search of excitement or escape. The objection is not so much directed toward the typical "comic" of the "respectable" sort found in the Sunday newspaper, though sometimes these, too, border on poor taste and dangerous fantasy. The real problem is the competition in portraying violent, fantastic, and sexually suggestive situations through drawings and texts. Nor is the menace confined to outright eroticism and pornography, for which the ordinary community in the average state has legal recourse. The overtones of sadism and sexual perversion are of even graver import, according to some who have studied the problem. While there is some difference of opinion as to how much "crime comics" have caused juvenile crime, no sane and disinterested person can claim that they have contributed anything to the spiritual growth or cultural development of the young people whose leisure is occupied with them. While there have been attempts to control or ban them by law, such laws must be drawn up carefully so as not to infringe on legitimate freedom of communication. In some communities, groups of parents and citizens have endeavored to work with merchants and vendors to evaluate such publications and secure voluntary removal of objectionable series. Sometimes, however, the merchant is himself at the mercy of wholesale distributors who require him to handle publications he does not want in order to get those he wants! Legislation banning such "tie-ins" may be of assistance to the conscientious newsstand operator.

The whole field of man's increasing leisure offers a lucrative opportunity for the unscrupulous exploiter. Many communities struggle with the problem of unsavory motion pictures. In the absence of state censorship—and we must remember that censorship threatens the occasional film with a provocative but unpopular idea as well as the morally doubtful products of the studios—alert policing can take care of the downright obscene film. Motion picture councils have rendered useful service in previewing and evaluating films. The most promising strategy would include solid education in the choice of amusements, use of reliable film estimates, a good variety of alternative recreational opportunities, and public opinion which avoids the evil *and supports the good* productions. *Martin Luther* amazed the movie critics in many cities because of the unexpected response it received. On the other hand, in one large city a well done film depicting a loved community servant did not last a week.

So, too, with television, radio, and other media, there must be intelligent, alert, articulate opinion brought to bear upon the right persons at the right time. Don't begin by "cussing out" the local station manager in the newspapers. Take it up with him if you saw something vulgar "get by." Let him know if a commentator was biased or a program unfair to a racial or religious group. Perhaps he needs just such an indication of consumer reaction to persuade the networks or the local producer that cheapness does not attract friends. And when there is something good, commend the station, the sponsor, the producer, or the network.

As for the long, loud, and "phoney" commercial, this is one of many brazen manifestations of the disregard of truth and good taste which has infected a large portion of modern advertising. So all-pervasive has become the pressure to "produce in order to consume in order to produce some more" that many caught in the whirl of advertising and selling will apparently do literally anything in order to "make a fast buck." Whether people can afford, need, or ought to have a given gadget, drink, or cosmetic does not enter into it. Whether the toothpaste will attract the paragons of success and good looks, or even do a decent job of cleaning the teeth, does not concern them. Whether the metal will hold up in the automobile engine or the aeroplane propeller is secondary to whether it can be sold! As Professor Albert T. Rasmussen has observed, "In our ethical climate, we have not become sensitive to the manipulative and organizational crimes that are probably far more serious to our social stability and morals than the clear-cut individual crimes of force and violence."[1]

Perhaps we feel less able to cope with this problem when we become aware of it. Yet we can work for the passage and enforcement of pure food laws and laws punishing false advertising. We can work to support organizations that help to inform and organize consumers. We can attempt to build up a moral climate in which truth and usefulness will again outrank profit and

---

[1] Albert T. Rasmussen, *Christian Social Ethics: Exerting Christian Influence*, p. 48. Prentice Hall, 1956.

"show." If nothing else, perhaps enough people can become angry enough to boycott the products of manufacturers that engage in the more outrageous practices. But even so, we shall recognize that a great deal of "influence peddling" does not meet our eyes, and we are taken in by many pressures we do not understand.

A particularly flagrant example of socially irresponsible pressure is the concerted effort to stimulate the sale and consumption of alcoholic beverages. Our annual expenditure for liquor is nearly ten billion dollars per year, more than we spend on milk and dairy products and four times as much as we spend on religion, welfare, and social service combined. The social costs of drink, in accidents, absenteeism, crime, medical care, and lowered efficiency, almost defy calculation. It is not likely that our country will again try to meet the problem by statutory prohibition of beverage alcohol. Contemplated laws, such as those prohibiting its use aboard aircraft or controlling liquor advertising, have their place and should be supported. But perhaps the chief responsibility of the church in this connection is to provide accurate information as to the nature of alcohol and the meaning of its use, and to labor for those personal and social changes which will reduce the desire for narcotic escape.

Discrimination

How do members of minority groups get along?

What racial, national, and cultural groups are represented?

Is there discrimination or segregation in schools, hospitals, courts, places of entertainment? Are there equal opportunities for housing, police protection, employment and advancement in employment?

Is there evidence of tension or misunderstanding between minority and majority group or between minorities?

What opportunities exist for interracial fellowship and cooperation in community concerns?

What minority groups are included in the membership, program, and outreach of your church?

One of the most deadly evils to be found in our society is race discrimination. It is found to some degree virtually everywhere, even in communities that think they are free of it. It exists flagrantly in certain southern states where White Citizens' Councils profess a doctrine of racial inequality which would have done credit to a Hitler and where the laws have prescribed segregated facilities. But in many northern states, too, Negroes find themselves unable to secure bank loans to purchase homes in "exclusive" neighborhoods or jobs as sales clerks, electricians, and engineers. Our cities frequently condemn minority group people to old housing in congested areas. But some small towns that pride themselves on having no race problem have nurtured this illusion by using one device or another to prevent Negroes, Puerto Ricans, or other non-white groups from taking up residence there! The community that has no minorities may thus actually have the worst problem of all, because it is unrecognized.

Discrimination takes many forms, and varies in degree. Until recent years the prevalence of lynching was a frightful reminder that, in certain sections of the South at least, Negroes had little security of life and person. Although there have been virtually no lynchings in the past few years (in the sense of deaths by mob violence), in a number of instances individual violence against Negroes has gone unpunished, as in the famous Till case where two white men won acquittal on a murder charge by claiming that they had kidnapped a Negro youth but later let him go! They were not even indicted for kidnapping!

Often, too, the Negro or other minority group person is at a disadvantage in the courts. Although federal judges have established a good reputation for integrity and courage and state courts are improving, some state courts and many local courts so fully reflect the prejudices of the dominant group in the locality that the Negro understandably believes that he "does not have a chance" when it is his word against that of a white man. This is especially noticeable in jury trials.

For many years the poll tax was a favorite means to prevent Negroes from voting. The threat of anti-poll tax legislation has led to the adoption of the "white primary" and other devices of doubtful constitutionality. Even within the same state practice varies, so that in one section the Negro's vote is allowed or even solicited, while in other areas intimidation may be used to prevent him from voting.

A serious problem, not confined to one region, is that of job opportunity. In many communities, Jews and re-

cent immigrants, no less than Negroes, may have difficulty in getting the better paying jobs for which they are
qualified, or in being upgraded on the same terms as
others.

Equal opportunities for housing, education, and recreation are other problems with which we become familiar as we study our community. Indeed, in virtually
every category of our survey we might well ask whether
any racial or cultural group is being excluded from the
rights and services to which all are entitled. Often the
pattern shows strange inconsistencies. In some communities, for example, Negroes may enjoy all public park facilities except the swimming pool, or be employed as
school teachers and policemen only in neighborhoods in
which Negroes are predominant. Jewish people, in turn,
have often had difficulty securing hotel accommodations
or admission into schools of medicine or law.

It is not surprising that the churches have been dis-
turbed by these violations of simple justice and brotherhood. From time to time during the last few decades denominational assemblies called for the correction of one
or another of these injustices. Gradually, however, it became apparent that standing behind many of these problems and reinforcing them, so that it was hard either to
recognize or remedy them, was the practice of racial segregation itself. White Protestants could live in the same
village with Americans of Japanese descent, Negroes, or
Jews; but if they never came into normal association, the
majority group would not even be aware of the disabilities to which their minority group neighbors were subjected. So, too, as long as schools, waiting rooms, rail-

road coaches, bus seats, and playgrounds were *separate,* the chances were that they would not be *equal.*

It is because of considerations such as these that the Supreme Court of the United States in May 1954 ruled that racial segregation in the public schools was unconstitutional and on its face discriminatory. The Federal Council of the Churches of Christ in America, later a part of the National Council of Churches, and many Protestant denominations had already denounced segregation during the 1940s. Most of the churches, even denominations whose strength lay in the South, commended the decision and called on their members to cooperate in putting the principle into practice. Similar court decisions have outlawed segregation in interstate buses and railroad coaches, in state universities, and in certain other facilities established by public funds. Many of these changes were accepted peacefully by the law-abiding majority of Southerners, so that by 1956 there were between 2,500 and 3,000 Negro students attending formerly white institutions of higher learning in the South. And when the Negro citizens of Montgomery, Alabama, protested the indignities to which they were subjected on the bus lines of that city, they won the sympathy and support of thousands of fair-minded people in the South as well as in the North.

There are many reasons why the fight against racial discrimination and segregation is crucial today. It is often pointed out that the prestige and good name of the United States as a leader among the free nations of the world is bound up with its assuring freedom and justice to its own citizens. This is especially acute at the point of race relations since three-fourths of the more than two billion people in the world are by our own definition identified with colored races. It is important, too, for the social health of our own nation that we should practice the democratic principles of responsible freedom and human dignity which we profess. What is more important, simple justice demands that every man be given access on equal terms to the necessities of life and the privileges which society offers. Above all, the Christian knows that in Christ all pride of self or race is ablished so that, seeing every man as a brother for whom Christ died, he can and must treat him as such. Whoever loves his neighbor as himself will find it intolerable that he should suffer the indignity and loss of freedom to which so many are subjected because of accident of birth.

What can Christians do? This question merits a volume in itself, but here is a beginning:

1. Keep informed. Get the facts and see that others have opportunity to get them, concerning tension, injustice, discrimination, and ways of dealing with them.

2. Take up with those having responsibility or influence locally the correction of discriminations in housing, schools, employment, recreation, and other services.

3. Foster associations across race lines, embracing many community interests, so that understanding and common objectives may be furthered.

4. Cooperate with public officials in complying with court orders, such as the public school decision. Where necessary, work for laws, on the federal, state, or local

level, to counteract discriminations which persist, as in employment.

5. Make certain that our own attitude and behavior toward members of minority groups is at least as courteous and fair as that we expect of public officials, employers, and other citizens.

In combating this as every other evil, the church may well pray in the words of Harry Emerson Fosdick's hymn—

> Save us from weak resignation
> To the evils we deplore;
> Let the search for Thy salvation
> Be our glory evermore.
> Grant us wisdom, grant us courage,
> Serving Thee whom we adore.[2]

These Churches Took Action

CASE A. Calvary Presbyterian Church, in Cleveland, Ohio, cooperated with neighboring Protestant churches and the auxiliary bishop in charge of the Roman Catholic church across the street in organizing the Hough Area Council. To stop the deterioration of the neighborhood householders were urged to repair and paint their property. Banks were encouraged to make loans for improvements. City inspectors cooperated by enforcing building codes. This effort, however, was limited because three inspectors had to cover an area of 70,000 people, and there was nowhere for many families to go if occupancy limits were strictly enforced. Besides broadcasting a Sunday morning service and making four neighbor-

---

[2] Copyright by Harry Emerson Fosdick. Used by permission.

hood canvasses each year, Calvary has offered its building for use by parole officers, Alcoholics Anonymous, paraplegic basketball players, and other community groups. During Lent its ministers and choirs take their turn conducting street-corner services from a rented truck to invite passers-by to the churches of the area. (Story in *Presbyterian Life,* April 14, 1956.)

CASE B. Several years ago ministers and other churchmen in Westmoreland County, Pennsylvania, aware that county officials were permitting gambling, vice, and racketeering, concluded that officials responsible for law enforcement were either involved in the criminal ring or had been bribed. They joined with other public-spirited persons in organizing Operation: Crusade, a movement which drew attention to the evil, brought about state police raids on some of the establishments, and drove others underground. Evidence of fraudulent balloting was also gathered, and candidates pledged to good government were encouraged to run for office. While their "slate" of candidates was not elected, several corrupt office holders were defeated and the public is becoming better informed about what is going on.

CASE C. The Kenwood-Ellis Community Church is located on Chicago's south side in an area which underwent rapid growth of population as older residents moved away and families displaced by land clearance projects moved in. Japanese-Americans and later Negroes added to the complexity of the area. The church serves its parish by visiting families in their crowded quarters, provides a nursery school for children, started classes in English for forgotten "foreigners," initiated a club program for children and teenagers. It housed the North-Kenwood-Oakland Community Conference and helped organize over five hundred families in Block Clubs to deal with the problems of delinquency, crime, adequate police protection, regular garbage collection, better lighting, and improved housing. The Conference has been especially alert in stopping illegal conversion of houses into multiple-family apartments and transient hotels. While other churches were closing their doors to the newcomers, Kenwood-Ellis, with an Evangelical and Reformed Nisei pastor and persons of various denominations in positions of leadership, added a Negro to its staff, and proceeded to enlist members from all racial groups.

CASE D. One of the significant experiments in ministering to urban congested areas is the group ministry of the East Harlem Protestant Parish, in New York City, and comparable programs in other cities. A unique feature is the cooperation of a single consecrated staff serving a half-dozen branches in as many different blocks. Among the problems encountered were poverty and unemployment; wretched housing and irresponsible landlords; high rates for tuberculosis, venereal disease, rat infestation, and infant mortality; lack of recreational facilities; crowded classrooms, juvenile delinquency and criminal gangs; use of narcotics by young boys and girls, family disintegration. Besides its programs of worship and Christian education in store fronts or other buildings as well as in churches where these are available, there are fellowship meetings of members living in a given tenement, discussion of needed political action, and persistent work with housing violations, delinquents, and so on. Street shows have been used to acquaint children and young adults with the effect of narcotics. (A fuller account of the program may be found in *The Church Serves the Changing City* by Ross W. Sanderson.)

CASE E. Fellowship House is an outgrowth of the Young People's Interracial Fellowship of Philadelphia. When leaflets and pamphlets attacking the Jews were widely distributed in 1938, the group was broadened to include members of the Jewish faith. Carefully trained teams including a white Christian, a Negro Christian, and a Jew, addressed schools, clubs, and church groups in the interest of good intergroup relations. When a transit strike crippled Philadelphia in 1944 because of the employment of Negroes as street-car motormen and conductors, Federal troops were sent into the city to operate the street cars and maintain order. The staff and members of the House, working with the Race Committee of the Society of Friends, the Jewish Community Relations Council, the National Association for the Advancement of Colored People, and other organizations, consulted with the police department, addressed meetings, and used other opportunities to reduce tensions and promote a settlement which assured equality in employment for all racial groups. (Reported by Fred D. Wentzel in *Once There Were Two Churches,* Friendship Press.)

CASE F. In 1954 a referendum on the legalization of bingo was put before the voters of Michigan. A number of social organizations and some churches supported the proposal. The state council of churches registered its opposition. A Christian citizens' committee, headed by a Presbyterian minister, put on an intensive campaign. A fund was raised to pay for radio and TV spot announcements and for leaflets. In many churches a message calling on their members to defeat the proposal was read to the Sunday morning congregation. The measure was defeated.

CHAPTER FIVE

There Are Causes to Be Supported

IN ITS dual role as servant and critic of the community, the church is obliged not only to fight the evils which may be evident but to support the constructive causes which make for the social and spiritual betterment of the entire populace. If the community needs a new hospital or an addition to the high school, it naturally looks to church people to back the movement to secure it. If there is a concern for mental health or for a planned parenthood clinic, for good government or for a better recreational program, one expects to find Prottestant church men and women among the sponsors. Red Cross and Community Fund campaigns, Boy Scouts and Four-H Clubs, Safety Week and Brotherhood Month —sometimes it seems that there are too many such causes. The responsible church will give its cooperation to those which are deserving, directing its strongest support to those which are most urgent—and perhaps least understood—in its own community at any given time.

Most of the areas on which our suggested survey has touched will at some time or other call for special effort. The congregation that is alert and organized for action will be prepared to lead or follow when such challenges come. At the same time it will take the initiative particularly in working for certain objectives, of value to every community, which the church is in an especially good position to see and to serve.

The Ministry of Reconciliation

Is there evidence of tension or misunderstanding between minority and majority group or between minorities?

What opportunities exist for interracial fellowship and cooperation in community concerns?

What minority groups are included in the membership, program, and outreach of your church?

One of the important functions of the church is to engage in the ministry of reconciliation. To be sure, when the New Testament speaks of Christ's work of reconciliation this involves first of all the restoration of fellowship between a man and God; but from this comes a reconciliation of a man with himself, and these two in turn make possible the reconciliation of man with man. Thus when the Letter to the Ephesians says of Christ that "he is our peace, who has made us both one," it is speaking in the context of the breach between Jew and Gentile which Christ has bridged. So Christ has brought together in himself men of many diverse racial and cultural origins. And it is the task of the church to give expression to this reality by being inclusive in its fellowship and in its ministry.

We have in the preceding chapter noted the seriousness of the racial injustice which mars and divides our
society and the obligation of the church to fight all discrimination based on race. It stands to reason that the
church's efforts for racial justice in the community will
be weakened in their effectiveness if the church is not
committed to brotherhood in its own life, and that its
testimony will be more convincing if its deeds support
its words.

It is a good sign that the church has had a troubled
conscience about its own behavior in this respect. The
disavowal of segregation by the then Federal Council
of Churches and by many denominations in 1946 and
subsequent years was directed against the church itself
as well as against the world. It called for "a non-segregated church and a non-segregated society." Both are
important, the latter from the standpoint of elementary
justice, the former from the standpoint of the church's
own integrity.

Progress in translating pronouncements into practice
is understandably slow. It is estimated that all but one-
half million of the seven or eight million Negro Protestants in the United States are members of Negro denominations. Such an historic situation is not overcome
quickly, yet a recent study by Dr. Alfred Kramer in
1952 showed that 9.8 per cent of the congregations in
three large denominations contained members belonging to more than one racial group. This is almost twice
the percentage noted by Frank S. Loescher in a study
of a larger number of churches made in 1946.

Most of the large and many medium-sized Protestant

denominations have social action agencies or race relations departments with staffs prepared to offer guidance
and assistance to congregations struggling with the questions of inclusiveness. We may get some direction from
the conclusions summarized by Dr. George G. Hack-
man, pastor of St. John's Lutheran Church in the Bronx,
at the time it made the transition from a "white" to an
inclusive fellowship. (See Case A on page 94.)

Go slowly, letting the growth be natural.

Attempt initially to obtain the support of the church
board if it can be done.

Count on losing a few families.[1]

Secure the services of a Negro worker in behalf of
the church, especially at the beginning.

Start with children. They have little prejudice to
overcome, and other important aspects of the plan
will stem naturally from admission of Negro children
to the educational program.

Build upon the religious resources which have been
developed over the years.

Preserve and employ the material and spiritual as-
sets of the church not only for a small interest group,
but for the service of the community in which the
church is located.[2]

---

[1] But note that according to Dr. Kramer's study only twenty-six persons out of the 237,000 members in those congregations that became inclusive withdrew their membership for reasons connected with the
church's racial policy.

[2] Quoted by S. Garry Oniki, "Interracial Churches in American
Protestantism," *Social Action*, January, 1950, p. 15.

Not every church may have the *opportunity* to welcome into its membership persons of races other than the majority group. No church, however, has a *right* to exclude such persons, and every church has a solemn *duty* to be prepared to minister to all who earnestly seek its fellowship. It must include people of all classes and conditions and ethnic backgrounds in its evangelistic effort. For an inclusive fellowship offers the strongest witness to the universal Christ, and the church that practices brotherhood is in the best position to battle for it.

Economic Justice and Integrity

What is the income range of the people?

How do they make their living?

What problems do they face in their daily work?

What is the relation between labor and management, businessman and consumer, farmer and townsman?

Is any economic group insufficiently represented in the leadership of the churches?

We have had several occasions to note the extent to which economic needs and economic relations affect our communities and the people within them "for weal or woe." Poverty, unemployment, lack of economic opportunity, and job discrimination lie behind many of the other difficulties from which persons suffer. The irresponsible use of economic power—and we might have added excessive economic privilege no less than want—

creates difficulties which cut deep into our society and destroy our moral fiber. In some areas the church has failed to reach a considerable portion of the population, especially at the levels of extreme wealth and extreme poverty; and there is a serious question how *deeply* its message influences the middle income groups with which, at least for the time being, religion appears to be enjoying a resurgence of popularity.

All of this means that the church must exercise wise leadership in relating its gospel to the practical problems of man's daily work and the ordering of our economic life in the interest of what the World Council of Churches has come to call a "responsible society." The local congregation that is aware of this can meet its responsibility and opportunity in several ways.

For one thing, it can help men and women, including youth, to find the meaning of their daily work from a Christian perspective and to make their vocational decisions from the standpoint of their Christian "vocation" or calling. There has been a gratifying rediscovery among the Protestant churches of the Protestant insight that all work that is valid at all has its relation to the will of God and our witness to Christ. This does not mean simply that church members are expected to use their associations and "contacts" at work in order to tell others about Christ or invite them to church. That is commendable if it is done with judgment and grace, but the Christian calling includes much more. It means that our work itself is held up to Christ for judgment, is offered to him in the spirit of worship, and becomes a channel through which God may meet the needs of our neighbors and maintain the peace and order of his world.

Many local councils of churches, and some local churches, have found it very helpful to follow the example of the National and the Canadian Councils of Churches which conducted a Conference on the Christian and His Daily Work in 1952. Theologians and laymen participated in interpreting what the gospel teaches about work, but the heart of the conference was discussion by groups made up of men and women who earned their living in one specific trade or profession. Bankers in one group, labor leaders in another, salesmen and executives, educators and physicians—each considered the responsibilities, the opportunities, the temptations, and the significance of his work from the perspective of the Christian conscience. In the local parish, too, preaching must be supplemented by personal counsel and such discussion; for finally, while the Christian experience of others can help, the person doing the job can best understand all that it involves and only he can make the final decision within the framework of the whole enterprise or profession of which he is a member.

Again, the local church has a concern for the relations between economic groups in the community—and, since in the modern world most communities are interlocked with most others, between economic groups across the nation and around the world. If town and country are at odds, the church may have a work of reconciliation to perform not by covering up conflicts or difficulties but by bringing farmers, consumers, business people, and industrial workers together to face their common problems within the framework of Christian fellowship and acknowledged social interdependence. If labor and management are suspicious of each other, the church might encourage members in both categories to come together to discuss their problem in the context of the whole problem of the economy. However, the church exercises this function best in "normal" times, rather than in the presence of a crisis such as the negotiation of a contract or the threat of a strike. Then lines harden and people on both sides are on the defensive.

This is not to say that the church may never perform a useful function during a crisis. There have been occasions when the representatives of the churches of a community helped to "soften" the conflict and bring about an agreement. More often, however, skilled negotiators and experienced mediators perform this function more effectively. The church can play a significant part in developing an atmosphere of mutual acquaintanceship, reliance on fair procedures, and an understanding of the ethical principles and assumptions which underlie a responsible economic society.

At the same time, the church cannot deal with the economic problems of the modern community as if it were benevolently neutral toward all claims and conflicts. Needless to say, it does not take sides in advance or "issue a blank check" to either management or labor, farm organization or processor in a dispute. But on some specific issues, if there is full information and careful checking of all facts and considerations, a church committee on Christian social action or community problems, a council of churches, or some responsible group of churchmen may well publicize its findings—provided it is not possible to work more effectively "behind the scenes" through consultation with both parties. This would be especially legitimate in instances of race discrimination on the part of either an employer or a group of employees; in the case of enterprises paying notoriously substandard wages; or in disputes based upon the denial of the right of labor to organize for purposes of collective bargaining.

On this last issue the major denominations in the United States have been on record for a half century. Many able interpreters of Christian social ethics would go farther and say that in a highly organized technological society like ours individuals have not only the *right* but the *duty* to join the labor union (or management group, farm organization, or professional association) through which the members of the group may advance their economic and social objectives, bargain, and cooperate with other groups. Yet many church members are scandalously ignorant of these facts and regard such organizations as evil. Though business and professional associations have come to be generally accepted, farm and labor organizations are often frowned upon, sometimes by members of other highly organized economic groups as well as by unsympathetic newspaper editors and columnists. The church has an obligation through its preaching, educational programs, and community outreach to make clear that it stands both for the right to organize and for the duty of the members of these organizations to make and keep them socially responsible.

Effective Citizenship

How is the community governed?

How fully do citizens participate in the processes of government?

Another cause in which Christian churches have a deep concern is that of effective citizenship. We have already considered some of the consequences when good government breaks down. The need of services which only the state can render adequately makes government a much more elaborate and indispensible factor in human experience than ever.

At this point we wish simply to underscore the importance of the *citizen* at all times and under all circumstances of community life. The more gigantic the structure of government and the more the dependence of the citizen on his government, the more the citizen is inclined to be overwhelmed by it. The greater, therefore, is the importance of his assuming a responsible relationship to his government at every level.

The church can assist this process in a number of ways. Certainly its preaching and teaching should help to create a desire in its members to participate in the responsibilities of citizenship. The stewardship of time and influence certainly implies our use of the privileges of civic and political life to work for a better community and world.

However, the individual has a right to expect more than exhortation and motivation. The fellowship of believers, if it takes its civic responsibility seriously, will strive to develop informed and effective citizens. It is not satisfied with banal "get out the vote" campaigns. It helps to secure the information and background which throws light on the issues and candidates. It seeks to acquire some "know how" about the political process, so that its members function in the precinct organization of their party and in the primary as well as in the general election. Such members will take account of the power structure of the community. They will use their influence where it counts and will offer thoughtful suggestions when ordinances and bills are being prepared in committee as well as urge their convictions when the final vote is being taken by the city council, the state legislature, or the Congress.

Finally, they will remain in touch with legislators and administrators so that they may be aware of new needs that emerge. Church people should not be satisfied to hop from stop-gap to stop-gap, necessary though this be. The church may well encourage long-range community planning which works years ahead in arresting blight and in anticipating needs. In smaller communities the social action committee of the congregation may keep in direct touch with such developments. In large metropolitan areas such relations may be more effectively maintained through the council of churches. But even in such centers, with all the resources available, many churches fail to utilize them.

Christians are citizens. They ought to be good ones. The church must help them to be such. For citizens who lack the training and tools of citizenship are as helpless as troops without weapons.

The Enlarging of Horizons

Is the community aware of the larger community?

Are its citizens informed of state, national, and international causes and appeals?

What organizations and institutions promote good citizenship, political action, and education about world affairs?

One of the most serious ailments from which any human being or institution can suffer is a constricted horizon. An individual whose vision and interest is limited to himself is hurting himself. A family that thinks so much of itself that it never thinks of other people is limiting itself and stunting the growth of its members. A community that lives to itself and shuts out any larger view wrongs both itself and the world.

In most communities there are evident links that connect it to the world beyond itself. The railroad and the highways carry commerce back and forth. The stores buy from outside, and the local farmers generally sell their produce to distant places. The gasoline station sells a nationally advertised brand, and the radio carries "network" programs originating in Bangkok or London. Taxes are paid to the Federal government, and young men may be summoned to military service in Korea or in Spain.

Yet amid all these evidences of interdependence, the people of a community may become smug and self-centered. All of these channels may serve merely for the convenience, the profit, the pleasure, or the security of

Main Street. Between elections we do not worry about Washington, and between wars we skip over the "foreign" news! In such circumstances, even a community that prospers economically may stagnate intellectually, socially, and spiritually.

The socially healthy community has many agencies to help prevent such self-isolation. Many labor unions, service clubs, and business groups have national and even international affiliations. There are voluntary associations, such as the League of Women Voters, foreign policy associations or world affairs study groups, organizations for better race relations, and social welfare councils, which bring national and international issues before at least a portion of the community regularly. The annual drives of the Red Cross and the organizations concerned with the conquest of various diseases remind us of our wider involvements. Observances like United Nations Week offer an opportunity to recall that we are citizens of one world and to dedicate ourselves to peace and good will.

Of all the institutions in the community, the Christian church is in the best position to remind men of their wider interrelations and their responsibility for those people and those interests which lie beyond their immediate view. For it directs them to their supreme loyalty. It speaks of a Christ who died to save the world. It lifts them to a perspective which takes in all men as their neighbors, and so includes the world in their horizon. And it is itself one part of a fellowship which goes beyond the limits of time as well as space to take in the faithful of every age and land.

So the church will continue to remind men of their common brotherhood with all men. It will by its special days call to their minds the importance of the effort to bring race relations, economic life, and the world community under the sovereignty of Christ and to make his love and justice determinative in all these areas. It will throughout the year carry on education and action on these problems, helping its members to understand them and deal with them as responsible citizens of God's world. Through its designated committees, councils, and assemblies the church will bear a corporate witness supporting policies which are beneficial to the whole world community, rebuking isolationism and narrow self-interest, and standing up for social righteousness in the concrete decisions which human institutions and governments are constantly making.

There is a principle stated in our Scriptures to the effect that "Every one to whom much is given, of him will much be required." This applies in a material sense to communities, groups, classes, and nations. It applies also, in terms of the riches of understanding, influence, and spiritual power, to the church. Of whom do God and man with better right expect a wise and courageous word when the civil rights and liberties of anyone are imperiled, when selfish or shortsighted groups would squander the natural resources of the people or use them for private gain, when the time has come to make our immigration policies more humane and just? Or who in this broad land has a clearer duty to work for the support of the United Nations, the control and constructive use of atomic energy, the extension and intensification of our efforts to "level up" the underdeveloped areas of the world through technical assistance and economic development?

The church has many resources. In addition to the publications and visual aids prepared by the United Nations and our own State Department, the churches themselves have prepared a variety of materials in many areas. The social action agencies of the various denominations, the Division of Christian Life and Work of the National Council of Churches, the World Council of Churches, the Commission of the Churches on International Affairs, and many private groups have resources of staff and program.

The denominational press carries many stories and statements concerning the Christian task in the world. Some congregations send their pastor or a lay leader to one of the denominational seminars in Washington or at the United Nations. Wise is the parish which has a social action committee to work with the pastor and the various auxiliary organizations to bring this information to its membership—by way of announcements, letters, posters, parish papers, forums, study groups, films, literature racks, and whatever means commend themselves for the situation, the problem, and the group to be served. The missionary program of the modern church has done wonders in broadening the vision of the man in the pew. The Christian approach to national problems and international affairs is doing much to fill in the big gaps on the map of the world between the outposts of denominational responsibility, so that we see in very truth that "the field is the world."

These Churches Took Action

CASE A. St. John's Lutheran Church in the Bronx has remained in its community through several succeeding waves of population change. When the first Negro children began to attend its Sunday church school it became aware that it had a mission to minister to them. So, when more Negroes moved into the area, it was prepared to serve them. Each year it continues to receive into membership a substantial number of both Negro and white children and adults. It has been aided in its ministry by the Lutheran Interracial Service which makes available a trained Negro social worker who not only interprets the church but also assists families with their own problems. Whether the area eventually becomes white, Negro, or mixed, the church thus has a strong nucleus of leaders prepared to continue its service to the community. (From an article by William A. Dudde in *The City Church*, March-April, 1953.)

CASE B. For a number of years certain churches in rural Vermont have invited Negro children from crowded Harlem to spend part of the summer on the farms of their members. This has given young people and adults in a completely white region opportunity to meet and live with children of another race, as well as giving these children a welcome change from crowded city living. At other times of the year, the young people from Vermont are guests of the families of these summer visitors in New York. Thus both groups give and receive in mutual fellowship.

CASE C. In New England the Methodist Church has

designated the Reverend Emerson W. Smith as a chaplain-at-large to industry. As such he visits factories to become acquainted with both management and labor people, addresses labor unions, and is occasionally called upon to counsel concerning personal problems or industrial relations.

CASE D. In Brookford, North Carolina, several years ago, the employees of a textile mill were attempting to organize a union to secure collective bargaining rights, better working conditions, and a more adequate wage. It was difficult for them to find a meeting place in the community, and many slanderous statements were made about the union and its purposes. The Evangelical and Reformed minister, however, agreed to speak over the radio interpreting the official statements of church bodies concerning the right of collective bargaining and interpreting the merits of the strikers. The minister and his church were sharply criticized by some persons identified with mill management, but he was able to maintain his witness to the Christian concern for justice and the democratic right to organize.

CASE E. In one Michigan community affected by a prolonged strike, the social action committee of the local Congregational Christian church asked both sides for information as to their point of view, grievances, and demands, and reported their findings. The fact that this church group showed its interest and that the chairman of the committee, though identified with the management of a firm not related to the strike, reported the issues fairly, was believed to have had some bearing upon a change in the readiness of one side to modify its terms and reach a settlement.

CASE F. In another midwestern community the ministerial association seeking to get accurate information on the issues in a telephone strike held a special meeting at which representatives of management and union were invited to speak and answer questions. In the course of discussion several matters came to light which had not been known or reported before, and a solution seemed possible. It is not known to what extent this meeting affected the negotiations, but it is significant that the leadership of the churches gave expression to its concern through intelligent searching for facts and discussion of issues.

CASE G. In several states Christian citizens have conducted Congressional District conferences in the interest of presenting the concern felt by church people for such matters as foreign economic aid, reciprocal trade agreements, and related international policies. Representatives in Congress—or during an election year the major candidates for Congress—are given a limited amount of time to present their basic convictions about foreign policy briefly and then exposed for a much longer time to the serious but friendly "give and take" of question and comment from the persons present. Needless to say, those who do the talking do well to study up on the subject—but the experience is enlightening for both Congressman and constituent.

CASE H. The First Presbyterian Church in Wappingers Falls, in the Hudson Valley, played host to eleven students from nine different countries, studying in New York City. The guests roomed, ate, played with the citizens of the community for three days, visited the local school, nearby industrial establishments, and points of interest in the vicinity. On Sunday they worshiped with their hosts at First Church. The hosts thus became acquainted with visitors from Chile, Japan, Egypt, while the visitors received a glimpse of life in American homes beyond the apartments of Morningside Heights. (Reported by *The Record,* Office of Educational Exchange—United States Department of State, January-February, 1951.) Similar weekend visits have been arranged by churches within convenient travel distance of New York for some of the "international civil servants" employed in the secretariat of the United Nations.

CHAPTER SIX

The Church Meets Its
Community Responsibility

WE HAVE been discussing some of the basic needs and problems to be found in almost any town or city in the land. Those existing in the reader's own community may not be identical with the examples selected, but there will be persons, needs, evils, and causes requiring attention; and if the student has followed the suggestions for exploration he should by this time have a fairly good idea of what they are.

All of this exploration and study, however, is preliminary to the main purpose which is—serving people, meeting needs, correcting evils, and bringing worthy causes to at least a partial triumph. Information is preparatory to action, particularly where human life and welfare are at stake. But first we must appraise the resources which exist for doing the job that has to be done.

Task and Resources

Who is meeting the existing needs of the community?

What are the organizations and institutions at work in the community?

What churches are there, and what are they doing?
In what ways do they cooperate in meeting community needs?

In every community there are agencies at work rendering the basic services on which people depend or meeting certain special needs. It is neither possible nor desirable that the church should itself dispense everything from penicillin to unemployment compensation, even though the church has a duty to see that these are not denied to anyone who has need of them. Social necessities and benefits, running the gamut from boys' clubs to chest x-rays, are provided by a variety of agencies, public and private. And if any of these is missing in any given locality, there is a variety of ways in which the need can be supplied.

1. *Government and various public agencies* are responsible for administering many of the fundamental social services. We look to local, federal, and state authorities for our water supply, traffic control, public schools, aid to dependent children, old age assistance, employment agencies, regulation of employment of women and children, soil conservation services, public health and sanitation, mental hospitals, as well as for police protection and civil defense. Eighty-five per cent of the twenty billion dollars we spend annually to provide for special social, economic and health needs comes through tax funds. The term "welfare state," used thoughtlessly or maliciously as a term of contempt by some critics, is actually a tribute to the kind of people and the kind of government that seek to serve the common good.

2. *Private welfare agencies and institutions,* administered by voluntary associations, also play a great part in serving human needs and furthering community improvement. Societies for the blind, family service agencies, community libraries, associations for mental health, and councils on human relations are but a few of the many organizations commonly called "secular" because they are independent of the control of any church, yet often organized by people who received their ideals and their motivation from the church if they are not prominent and active leaders in the churches.

3. *Some of these agencies and institutions will be sponsored by and directly related to the churches of the community,* or the churches of a particular denomination or group of denominations. Thus there are Methodist and Lutheran hospitals, Presbyterian children's homes, Episcopal community centers, Baptist homes for the aged, and Protestant interracial fellowships. Hospitals and much of modern social work had their beginning within the church. Although the church has neither the reason nor the capacity to take all these services back under its wing, there will continue to be a place for the church-related hospital and case-work agency as a corporate witness to the church's obedient and loving concern for the total good of the total person.

4. *Some phases of the church's social ministry will be carried out by the churches working cooperatively.* It may be by a group of churches in a given neighborhood providing together a program for young people or for the aging, which none of them could offer alone. Thus one church may undertake a special ministry for the youth of a community. Another may house a day nursery for small children. A third may offer its facilities to a "golden age" group. Or it may be that a council of churches is the best agency through which to assist a juvenile or a domestic relations court on behalf of all Protestant and Orthodox congregations. An interchurch committee on public affairs can secure adequate and accurate information on issues or candidates in an election, when the members of a single congregation would be limited to the experience and perspective of one district, one political persuasion, or one economic class. Even in so simple a matter as dividing an urban neighborhood into districts for evangelistic followup and pastoral service, five or six churches may agree which will be primarily responsible for the unchurched in which blocks. And when it comes to focussing attention on bad housing, race discrimination, or an important piece of legislation, a cooperative strategy making use of every voice and every available worker is far more effective than the scattered, hit-or-miss approach of divided Protestantism.

5. *Despite these many resources, nothing can take the place of the local church itself.* There are some services that no one else can render for its people or its parish. The joint efforts of the community's churches will be ineffective unless there is a strong base of cooperation and support in each of the congregations in the area. And the community will be best served if there is understanding and cooperation between each church and the private agencies working for the health, welfare, decency, and harmony of the whole.

The Role of the Local Church

At Cleveland, Ohio, in November, 1955, the National Council of Churches convened a National Conference on the Churches and Social Welfare. One of the sections of this conference considered the responsibility of the local church to engage "both alone and cooperatively with other congregations" in a social ministry. It noted seven functions, listed here with brief comments by the present writer.[1]

1. *"To interpret to its members the Christian basis of the church's social concern and the dimensions of its task."* The church has a great heritage, extending back to the Old Testament Law, the teaching of the prophets, and the ministry of our Lord. Too many of its present-day members, however, do not understand the biblical and theological principles underlying its concern for human suffering and social problems or the story of the modern reawakening to the importance of this response to the love of Christ.

2. *"To study the community, its needs and resources, with a sensitivity to the needs of people and a sense of its mission in the community."* This assumes that a responsible group or committee in the church will continue to scrutinize

---

[1] Report of Section F-2, "Social Education, Action, and Research," in *Churches and Social Welfare,* Vol. III, "The Emerging Perspective," p. 107, E. Theodore Bachman, Editor. National Council of Churches, 1956.

the kinds of situations and resources which have been pointed up in this present study.

3. *"To cooperate with welfare agencies, private or public, in meeting the needs which exist—enlisting support, participating in community social planning, encouraging qualified members to serve in agencies or on their boards and assisting in the recruitment and training of personnel for such agencies."* Often the leaders in our churches do not realize how significantly their ministry and influence can be extended by the services of trained and consecrated Christians working as board members, volunteers, or paid staff in community organizations. Sometimes church officers even begrudge the time a pastor or a member may devote to such causes, instead of rejoicing that his time and ability are being used. The church should, rather, hold up the significance of teaching, social work, and service in the interest of organizations devoted to human relations or economic improvement, as Christian vocations. It is especially important that the church be officially represented on the community or area council. This will both express the church's own commitment to community good and bring to its membership continued information as to the needs of the community and the kinds of action required.

4. *"To stimulate the extension of existing agencies, public or private, or the creation of new ones to meet unsolved problems."* As new problems emerge or existing needs are found to be inadequately served some arrangements must be made either to assign the responsibility to an established agency or to set up a new one. The average

church is not in a position to decide which choice should
be followed. Its representatives are, however, well equipped to call attention to the lack and to consult with
other churches, with community leaders, and with other
agencies through a social planning council or clearing
house for the filling of the gap.

5. *"To engage in service projects where such action is most
promising."* The stories of churches which have in various
ways accepted the challenge of their community illustrate some of the kinds of projects which might be considered. Naturally, the nature of the endeavor will be
conditioned by the type of people and need prevailing,
the resources and facilities of the church, and the presence or absence of other agencies performing the specific kind of task under consideration. It is not too
much to say, however, that every church has the obligation to serve its neighborhood as it is able. Such service may be an individual, personal ministry as when
its pastor is available for counsel to all comers. It may
mean a few regular weekly activities such as scout troops,
or an occasional public meeting under the sponsorship
of the community council. Or it may be a highly organized group-work program administered by a full-time
staff. Whatever the form its projects take, the important
point is to find practical expression for the conviction
that the church is here because it has a mission *here*.

6. *"To inform the membership of the position of denominational and interdenominational councils on questions of
public policy."* If many members are vague about the
social teachings of the Bible and the church's response

to human need through the centuries, they are almost completely illiterate when it comes to the official statements and social teachings of representative church bodies today. Every major denomination including his own had for many years been on record as condemning racial segregation on biblical and theological grounds; yet a Protestant minister was widely quoted as stating contemptuously that nobody had questioned the moral rightness of segregation until the Supreme Court outlawed it in the public schools! If a clergyman can be so ill-informed about the widely publicized pronouncements of his own church, it is perhaps not surprising that many laymen remain ignorant of the growing body of counsel on social questions which has been produced by the churches. Yet the resolutions of one's own denominational assemblies as well as the results of discussion between representatives of many confessions and points of view in the National and World Councils of Churches can be easily secured from their respective headquarters.[2]

7. "To take action on questions of legislation or public policy affecting the common welfare." If the function of the church is both to promote the total good of the total society and to hold up all decisions and institutions to critical judgment, it has a responsibility not only to serve within the framework of existing institutions but to speak when basic policy decisions are being made. A decision at City Hall may cut relief and undermine ad-

---

[2] See address of latter in list of national agencies in the appendix, page 117. For denominational statements write to main office or social action agency of your own denomination.

vances achieved by churches and social agencies after years of effort. A pending bill in the state legislature may set up standards of child care which will have a more far-reaching effect than all the work of child-care institutions under the direction of the church. A telegram in time may arouse an uninformed, uncertain, or merely busy Congressman to the importance of an appropriation for the United Nations technical assistance program. Increasingly the church, at every level, must be prepared to act, intelligently and at the right time, in the shaping of political decisions affecting our community and ultimately every community in the world.

Your Church and Its Resources

Before proceeding to formulate some suggestions for the future planning of his own congregation, the student should review its present program and ask himself: What has our church done to serve these community needs? How is it now helping to improve the quality of the services on which all depend? How is it helping to assure the kind of government, health, recreation, and welfare services that are needed? What is it doing to combat discrimination and other social evils? In what definite ways does it enlarge the interests and horizons of its constituents and enlist them to take part in social action for a better community, nation, and world?

Then it becomes necessary to appraise the resources at the command of the individual congregation. Does it have the sort of building, facilities, and leadership which could carry on an expanded community program if such is needed? For example, its available meeting rooms may be well adapted to the activities of children or "golden agers" but not satisfactory for a teen canteen. In some instances, remodeling or expansion of plant is advisable. In others this is impossible.

Again, is its membership large enough and potentially able to contribute enough to launch an extended and expensive service program, or does a more modest effort seem more realistic? This question should not be prejudged, however; for many churches have not begun to tap their material resources, and service programs have a way of awakening new loyalty and support. Or, in the presence of genuine need for which after an honest effort the strength of the parish is insufficient, additional support may be forthcoming from local denominational associations and presbyteries, or from national home mission boards.

In any case, what are the future trends of membership, giving, community changes, and social needs? Often councils of churches, denominational research departments, city planning commissions, chambers of commerce, or social planning councils can give valuable guidance here.

Getting Under Way

Having considered such factors as the nature of the community and its needs, the resources which there are for meeting them, the existing program and resources of your own church, a congregation can now face the $64,000 question.

What is our community responsibility?

In the light of the available information and the resources at our disposal, what is our obligation?

What specific ministry shall our congregation explore further and undertake now?

At the heart of any program of community service and social action there must be a *commitment* on the part of the members of the church. They need to consecrate themselves and their church again and again for such a complete witness that their activity in political party, labor union, or welfare agency becomes an expression of the life of the church and their own life in Christ. This service will be nourished by the corporate worship of the fellowship and brought under the searching scrutiny of God's Word; and it will in turn give vitality to the entire work and worship of the congregation.

A second essential, pointed out by a report from which we have already quoted, is *"an inner Christian integrity* which expresses itself in a community-wide inclusiveness transcending limitations of race, culture, and class."[3] Such a church is best able to function in the interest of welfare and justice and least likely to confuse the class interests of its members with the will of God for the world.

A third essential is *effective organization.* While a program of outreach and service and social witness should involve the entire congregation, responsibility for the formulation of plans and administration of pro-

---

[3] *Churches and Social Welfare,* Vol. III, p. 107 (Emphasis supplied).

grams undertaken by the congregation is ordinarily best delegated to a committee. This may be a special committee chosen for a particular project. Or it may be a standing committee on social action, public affairs, community relations, or social welfare. Indeed, even when a project becomes big enough to require a special committee, the church's many social concerns should be coordinated by a single committee, or at most two central committees responsible for local service projects and for social education and action respectively. Thus the Cleveland Conference's Section on Social Education and Action advised:

> In giving expression to its concern for welfare agencies on the one hand and for social education and action on the other, the congregation is faced with the problem of integrating its interest and activity, so that confusion of aims and waste of resources are avoided. A single committee responsibile for both community outreach and social education, or frequent consultation where two separate committees exist, would be imperative.[4]

How does a church get such a committee under way? That, naturally, depends upon the church and upon the situation. In some cases, a current need makes it almost inevitable to appoint a committee—a challenge to adopt a refugee family; a desire to get action on housing or foreign aid; a denominational or interdenominational emphasis on Christian vocation or on world order.

Some churches face the question when they revise or rewrite an outmoded constitution. What is more logical than to analyze the church's structure in terms of its

---

[4] *Ibid.*, Vol. III, p. 107.

functions, and so to make provision for committees to spearhead all the basic responsibilities—Christian social action along with evangelism, Christian education, and the rest?

Some churches, however, require more deliberate cultivation. Suppose only the minister or a few hardy souls see the need of a community program and a committee to help the church fulfill its social role. In one instance, the pastor may invite a member of his denominational social action staff to occupy the pulpit and to meet key leaders in the church around the dinner table afterward. In another case, a social action film might be presented at a church night supper, to arouse interest in the needs of the community and a program to meet them.[5] In some cases, the initiative may have to be taken by an existing organization or by a voluntary group formed for the purpose of Christian social action.

Ordinarily, however, a committee on social action and community service would be appointed by the council, session, consistory, or official board of the congregation. Or it might be elected at the annual congregational meeting. Its members would include persons with experience and competence in the various areas with which such a committee deals—economic life, citizenship, race relations, international affairs, and selected aspects of social welfare. It might include people identified with a local college or university, a high school teacher, a county agricultural agent, or a labor union officer. It should certainly include the appropriate persons responsible

---

[5] See suggested visual aids on pages 121, 122.

for social action and community outreach in the men's, women's, and youth organizations of the church. Indeed, where these auxiliaries participate in a vital denominational program, they often provide the spark for an all-church effort.

How Does it Work?

What does such a committee do? If it is wise, it will begin by *organizing and orienting its own members* in their specific tasks; they may devote several meetings to study of the local church's social function and the program of the denomination in social action. It may divide its members into subcommittees on social welfare, economic life, race relations, international affairs, and other concerns. This will pinpoint responsibility for investigation and study, for referral of requests coming to the church from denominational and community agencies, and for drafting recommendations to the group as a whole.

One of the first things will be to establish some priorities, to select among all the known needs and causes those which are most urgent, for which least is being done, and which the church is in the best position to serve; to agree as to which projects ought to be undertaken this year, and which might be considered later; which community campaigns and causes are most in need of volunteers or financial assistance; which agencies in the field of civil rights merit confidence and cooperation; which legislative proposals merit strong support, and when.

The committee will seek ways of *keeping its members*

informed. Local and denominational agencies, as well as the organizations and printed resources listed in the appendix of this book, will be helpful. Some members of the committee, particularly women with time to invest, could attend important meetings of local governmental bodies, participate in community organizations, or investigate social conditions at first hand.

Then, the committee will devise ways of *getting the attention of the congregation and keeping it informed.* Notices in the parish paper, announcements in the Sunday bulletin, clippings and posters on the bulletin board, the literature rack, and the reading table are all useful allies. Forums, panel discussions, field trips, plays, audio-visual aids—these can be used well to inform and arouse to action.

But the point is *action.* As we have assumed throughout this study, knowledge and action cannot be separated. Since the action required is frequently determined by the problem and the situation, we have in each of the preceding chapters offered a few case studies in the hope that these would be more helpful than rigid rules in stimulating the consecrated ingenuity which is essential. To these may be added a few examples of ways in which churches can act.

Sometimes a need can be met by *purposeful giving* to an established cause—as when a church contributes to a children's home or to the defense of the victims of racial injustice. Sometimes a church can participate directly in a *project,* such as the sponsorship of a refugee family or a boys' club.

Sometimes the church can function best through *quiet*

intervention, as when it seeks to assure equal service for members of minority groups in barber shops or restaurants by consulting with the management. Sometimes, if such reasoning does not work, it may be necessary to resort to *public protest or demonstration,* as when church youth groups picketed establishments which persisted in discriminating.

In some instances the social action committee, or the officers of the local church, have made a *formal appearance before governmental bodies,* as in opposing the licensing of a tavern near a school or a church, or to request the opening of public recreational facilities to persons unjustly excluded on grounds of race. In other instances, churches have found a more elaborate strategy necessary and have cooperated with other public-interest groups in the *use of mass media* and *organized pressure* to secure approval of slum clearance and low-cost housing projects.

On some occasions, church social action committees have found it effective to secure signatures to *resolutions* and *formal petitions* requesting legislative action. A conspicuous example of this was the movement to secure approval of the United Nations charter. Carefully thought-through resolutions on matters of public policy are always valuable. But they are best supported by *thoughtful letters individually written* and directed to their representatives and officials by the members of the churches whose official bodies have adopted them. Ten thousand personal appeals for increased technical assistance funds would be ten times as effective as ten times as many signatures on form letters!

So a responsible committee can be an important part of the church's witness—sometimes taking action on its own, sometimes helping the members of the church to act; now stimulating service projects, now turning them over to others; expressing the felt needs of the congregation, yet persistently bringing before the congregation the needs of which it may not yet be fully aware.

With the help of such a committee, the church can engage in a continued study of its responsibilities and opportunities; can be given representation on various community councils and agencies; can be kept informed of important developments in local and national politics calling for citizen action; and can project its objectives and activities with a knowledge of what it is doing and with some hope of effectiveness.

Good organization will also make possible effective coordination within the church itself. If the social action departments of the lay groups are represented on the church's social action committee as suggested above, their efforts will reinforce each other instead of competing; one group will be less likely to set up a program in ignorance of what others are planning; and it will be possible for the church to give a clear corporate witness in the community.

Effective coordination will mean harmony with the other interests and activities for which the church is responsible. The community outreach in service and the community outreach in evangelism will be coordinated so that conflict or confusion may be avoided. Social education will be related to the other phases of the church's total effort at Christian education. The church's interest in missions and in overseas relief or world service will be seen in relation to its efforts in behalf of world community through political action and education in international relations.

Again, wise organization will keep before the church the reminder that a church cannot and ought not try to do everything alone. It will remain in communication with its denominational agencies for social action and social welfare. It will work closely with the local council of churches, and if there is no such organization it will create some means for coordinating church effort.

Finally, a good committee will remember that the best organization in the world is not an end in itself. It is a necessary means to a larger end. The real aim will be kept in mind—that the church may fulfill its calling as the servant of the most humble and the prophetic critic calling even the most exalted to judgment, so that every community may take on something of the quality of *Christian* community life.

Here they stand: your church and your community! May each strengthen the other. And may both serve God's people as he intends.

Suggested Resources

Agencies

AFTER LOCAL and denominational resources have been tried, it will be profitable to get in touch with some of the following agencies:

ACTION (American Council to Improve Our Neighborhoods)
P. O. Box 462, Radio City Station, New York 20, New York

Alcoholics Anonymous
P. O. Box 459, Grand Central Annex, New York 17, New York

American Association for the United Nations
345 East 46th Street, New York 17, New York

American Federation of Labor and Congress of Industrial Organizations
815 Sixteenth Street, N.W., Washington 6, D. C.

Family Service Association of America
192 Lexington Avenue, New York 16, New York

League of Women Voters
1026 Seventeenth Street, N.W., Washington 6, D. C.

National Association for the Advancement of Colored People
20 West 40th Street, New York 18, New York

National Association for Mental Health, Inc.
1790 Broadway, New York 19, New York

National Conference of Christians and Jews
43 West 57th Street, New York 19, New York

National Consumers' League
348 Engineers Building, Cleveland 14, Ohio

National Council of Churches of Christ in the U.S.A.
  Division of Christian Life and Work
  297 Fourth Avenue, New York 10, New York

  Division of Christian Education
  257 Fourth Avenue, New York 10, New York

  Church World Service
  215 Fourth Avenue, New York 3, New York

National Education Association of the United States
1201 Sixteenth Street, N.W., Washington 6, D. C.

National Health Council, Inc.
1790 Broadway, New York 19, New York

National Housing Conference
1025 Connecticut Avenue, N.W., Washington, D. C.

National Social Welfare Assembly
345 East 46th Street, New York 17, New York

National Urban League
1133 Broadway, New York 10, New York

United States Department of Health Education and Welfare
Washington 25, D. C.

World Council of Churches (U.S. Office)
156 Fifth Avenue, New York 10, New York

Books

Bachman, E. Theodore (editor) *The Emerging Perspective.*
Volume III of *Churches and Social Welfare,* National Council of Churches, 1956. Contains complete report of National Conference on the Churches and Social Welfare, November, 1955.

Bennett, John C., *Christian Ethics and Social Policy*. Scribner, 1946. An excellent interpretation of how the Christian faith and ethic can be related to the concrete problems of social and political action.

Cook, Clair M., *The Modern Samaritan*. Board of Social and Economic Relations of the Methodist Church, 1956. A compact guide to problems of Christian social action, particularly useful in its discussion of economic and race relations.

Crain, James A., *Christian Action and Community Service*. Coordinating Council, Disciples of Christ. A manual for the guidance of a local church committee on Christian service. While planned for Disciples Churches, it contains information useful to all.

Klemme, Huber F., *The Bible and Our Common Life*. Christian Education Press, 1953. A study of the social teachings of the Bible, which underlie the Christian concerns discussed in the present course.

Krumbholz, Clarence E., *Christianizing Community Life*. Muhlenberg Press, 1951. A thirteen-lesson course on the church's community responsibility by the executive director of the Division of Welfare of the National Lutheran Council.

Kuhn, Margaret E., *Houses and People*. National Council of Churches, 1956. A study guide on the problem of housing and what can be done about it.

Leiffer, Murray H., *The Effective City Church*. Abingdon-Cokesbury, 1949. A standard guide for the development of church programs in terms of the nature and need of the urban community.

Rasmussen, Albert T., *Christian Social Ethics: Exerting Christian Influence*. Prentice Hall, 1956. A helpful analysis

of the social responsibility of the church and the problem
of its effectiveness in the local community, in daily work,
and in political life.

Sanderson, Ross W., *The Church Serves the Changing City*.
Harper, 1955. Case studies of a number of city churches,
eight treated in detail, which in various ways are seeking to
minister to the city's needs.

Seifert, Harvey, *The Church in Community Action*. Abingdon-Cokesbury, 1952. One of the best guides for organizing
the church and developing a program of social education
and action related to the local parish situation.

Smith, Rockwell, *The Church in Our Town*. Abingdon-
Cokesbury, 1945; revised 1956. Guidance for the town and
country church in understanding the rural community and
ministering to it effectively.

The Church and the Community. Department of Social
Education and Action, Presbyterian Church in the U.S.A.
An instructor's manual for studying a church's community
responsibility. Very helpful suggestions for guiding discussion and an especially good treatment of the social structure
of the community.

Warren, Roland L., *Studying Your Community*. Russell
Sage Foundation, 1955. Probably the most complete outline
for study of the community, with detailed questions and
references to books and agencies related to the various social areas.

Webb, Muriel S., *The Social Ministry of the Local Church*.
Department of Social Welfare of the National Council of
Churches, 1956. A study guide on the local church's social
outreach, based upon the message and selected emphases of
the National Conference on the Churches and Social Welfare.

Wentzel, Fred D., *Once There Were Two Churches*. Friendship Press, 1950. A treatment of church responses in various types of situations rural and urban, enriched by illustrations and devotional materials.

Magazines

A Christian Newsletter on International Affairs. Department of International Affairs, National Council of Churches, 297 Fourth Avenue, New York 10, New York. 12 issues per year, $1.00.

Christianity and Crisis. 537 West 121st Street, New York 27, New York. Bi-weekly, $3.00 per year.

The City Church. Department of Urban Church, National Council of Churches, 257 Fourth Avenue, New York 10, New York. Bi-monthly except July and August, $2.00 per year.

Information Service. Bureau of Research and Survey, National Council of Churches, 297 Fourth Avenue, New York 10, New York. Weekly except July and August, $2.50 per year.

Interracial News Service. Department of Racial and Cultural Relations, National Council of Churches, 297 Fourth Avenue, New York 10, New York. Bi-monthly, $2.00 for two years.

Memo. Washington Office, National Council of Churches, 122 Maryland Avenue, N.E., Washington 2, D.C. Semi-monthly except August and September, $1.00 per year.

Social Action. Council for Social Action, Congregational Christian Churches, 289 Fourth Avenue, New York 10, New York. Nine issues per year, $2.00.

Social Progress. Department of Social Education and Action Presbyterian Church in the U.S.A., 830 Witherspoon Building, Philadelphia 7, Pennsylvania. Monthly except July and August. $1.00 per year.

Visual Aids

First Church Serves Its Community. Filmstrip with recorded sound. Department of Social Welfare, United Christian Missionary Society, 222 S. Downey Avenue, Indianapolis 7, Indiana. Shows how a congregation became aware of the problems of its city and began to deal with them.

Sound of a Stone. 28 minute sound motion picture, color or black and white. Board of Social and Economic Relations, The Methodist Church, 740 Rush Street, Chicago 11, Illinois. Dramatic film showing how gossip and hysteria threaten the good name of an individual and the freedom of the school.

A Train of Action. 28 minute sound motion picture in color. Bureau of Audio-Visual Aids, Evangelical and Reformed Church, 1505 Race Street, Philadelphia 2, Pennsylvania. Narrative film depicting the development of a community consciousness and outreach on the part of a conventional church.

What Happened to Hannah? Cartoon filmstrip on the social ministry of the local church. 75 frames with sound. Department of Social Welfare, National Council of Churches and denominational visual aid departments.